SHOOTS

A Guide to Your Family's Photographic Heritage

Thomas L. Davies

Addison House
Danbury, New Hampshire

ISBN 0-89169-012-3

Designed by Logowitz + Moore Associates

Typeset by Typesetting Service Company
in Linotype Fairfield

Printed by Halliday Lithograph

For My Family

Introduction

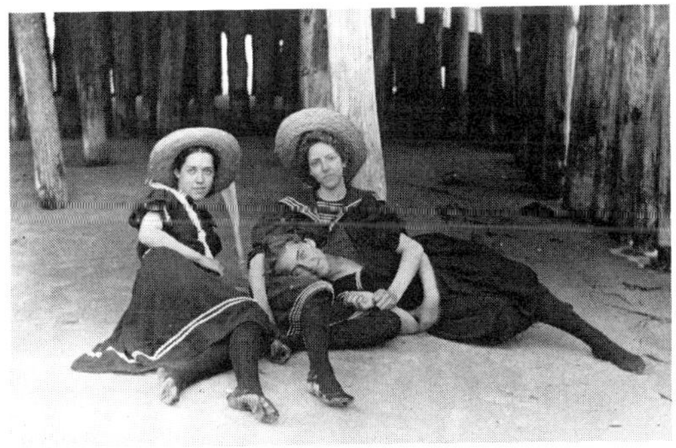

In this age of disposable everything, we must be careful not to dispose of our past. It seems that as our world speeds up, more artifacts are left behind. Every time we move from one place to another, we shed a piece of our heritage. This book came about as a result of my concern that the home archives be passed on to future family, friends, and historians. ▣ Photographs comprise one of the richest and most portable parts of our past. Properly preserved and organized, a collection of family pictures will take up no more space than an average suitcase and can last for hundreds of years. Moreover, photographs from the past have a sense of immediacy about them; they are a time machine, *a window into the past.* ▣ Photographs are especially delicate things. They are most commonly pieces of paper that will crack, tear and disintegrate under adverse conditions. *Modern plastic album pages will eventually destroy your family snapshots.* Easily shattered glass negatives and combustible nitrate negatives can still be found in attics. Closer to home, color slides and color prints will fade much more quickly than black and white photographs. ▣ Now is the time for family photographers and historians to come to the aid of their own photographic heritage. It is no small task to find, organize, restore and preserve a collection of photographs, but if it is not done, a valuable legacy

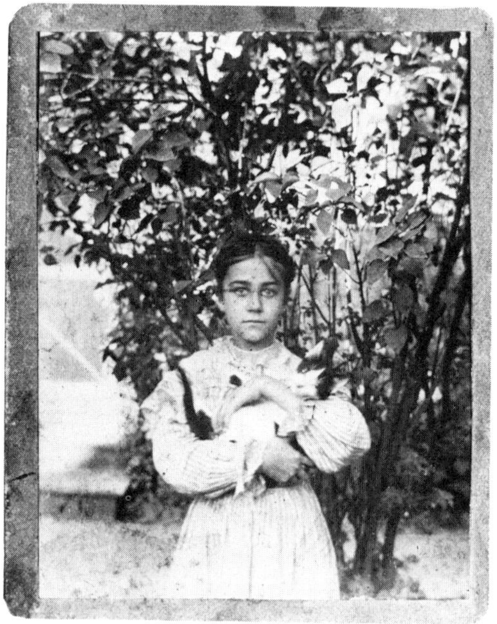

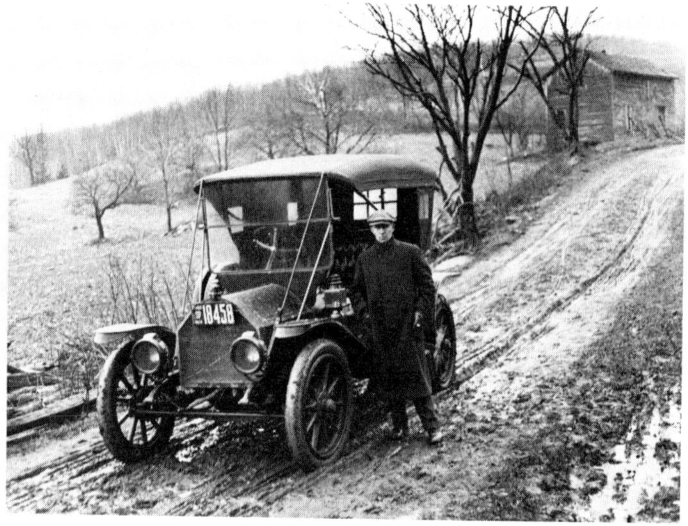
18458

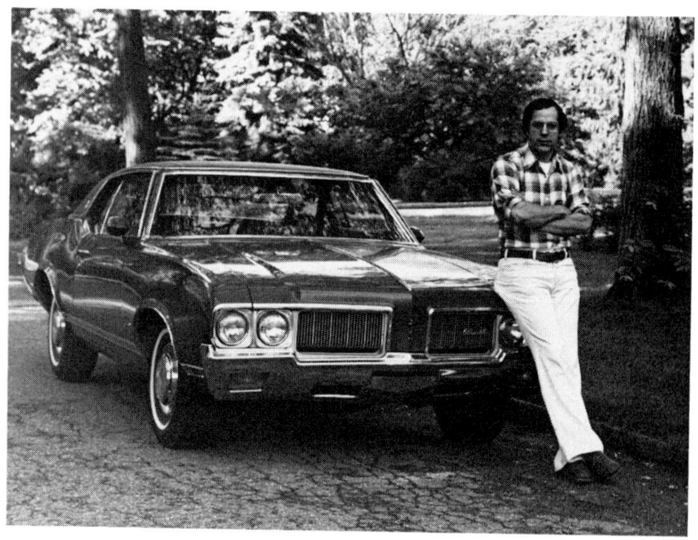

will be lost. We must establish a new tradition of the family photo-historian. It is a great deal of work, but once done, you will know your ancestors with an intimacy not easily accomplished with the written word. Our best photographs can tell us more than the most detailed genealogy about the people who have been members or close friends of our family. ▣ While delving into your family's past, you might consider leaving more than a few traces for future generations. In looking at the old photographs, it is not the great event – everyone lined up at graduation – that holds our interest. Rather, it is grand father fishing or great-grandmother holding a kitten when she was six that fascinates us. Small details become vital facts. *We can learn from the past how to make photographs for the future.* Very ordinary photographs are capable of becoming extraordinary with nothing more than the passage of time. Look, for instance, at two typical person-next-to-the-car photographs. The first one, made in 1914, is most fascinating today. The two spare tires, the man's heavy overcoat buttoned against the winter, the rutted road, these and other parts of the picture hold our attention. What was commonplace in 1914 is rare today. The other picture, taken in 1977, has virtually all of the components of the first one, but is not nearly as fascinating to us. I am certain, however, that in the year 2040, people looking at this picture will be amazed by the size of the car, if nothing else. Because we can see more clearly at a distance of 75 years, many of the photographs illustrating this book date from the turn of the century. By studying them and by considering your yet unborn audience, you will develop an entirely new way of photographing your family today. ▣ Your collection of photographs may be limited to the pictures you've made in the last two years. That's not much history, but if you begin identifying, organizing and preserving your photographs now, your collection will be much more valuable to your great-great-grandchildren when they make their historic discovery one hundred years from now. It is up to you and someone in each future generation to make sure this will be possible.

I
Location of Family Photographs: Places to Look, People to Ask, and Things to Look for

You no doubt have a pretty good idea where your family's photographs are kept, but remember to check with your relatives. Often they will have collections of photographs that you can borrow long enough to make copies. Most people are delighted to have extra prints of family photographs. Older relatives are also probably your only source for identifying the people who appear in the earlier pictures. ▣ While the usual attics and cellars will no doubt hold many of your family's photographs, don't forget garages, closets, drawers, barns, desks, bookcases, suitcases, as well as books and yearbooks – wedding and anniversary albums, too. ▣ You might also consider contacting the Mormon Church. In Utah, drilled into a mountainside, the Mormons have the largest genealogical archive in the world. There is a very good chance that, whether you're a Mormon or not, some of your ancestors' photographs are on microfilm in Salt Lake City. Check with your local branch library of the Mormon Church; they're very helpful. ▣ If you are having photographs sent to you, instruct the sender in the proper way to pack prints. They should be wrapped in heavy paper and placed in a polyethylene bag. The bag is then taped securely to the *center* of a much larger piece of sturdy cardboard or masonite. Another piece of board is placed over the photographs and this rigid bit of construction is then wrapped in more heavy paper. If the package is large, it may be shipped in a sturdy shipping box. ▣ When it comes to judging the historical merit of your more recent photos, don't be too hasty in your decisions as to which ones should be kept. The best way to evaluate contemporary photographs is to calmly put yourself 50 or 100 years into the future and look objectively at the pictures. This is easier if you start by looking at the photographs we have chosen to include in Chapter VI. What *is* fascinating to you? Usually it is the clothing and the hairstyles that strike you first. Old interiors, automobiles and other pieces of the scene are also very important. The newer pictures probably have much the same information; it is just too close to you now to seem interesting. *Put yourself in the twenty-first century when you edit your collection.* ▣ As you go through your photographs, you will want to establish the dates they were made. Information in the picture itself, such as license plates, calendars, posters, etc., will give you some clues. Another way is to ascertain what process was used to make the photograph. A list of processes (with the years in which they were produced) follows that might help you identify and date some of your earlier photographs.

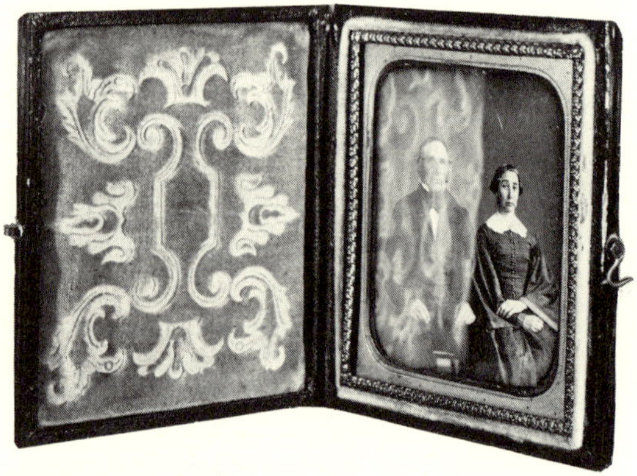

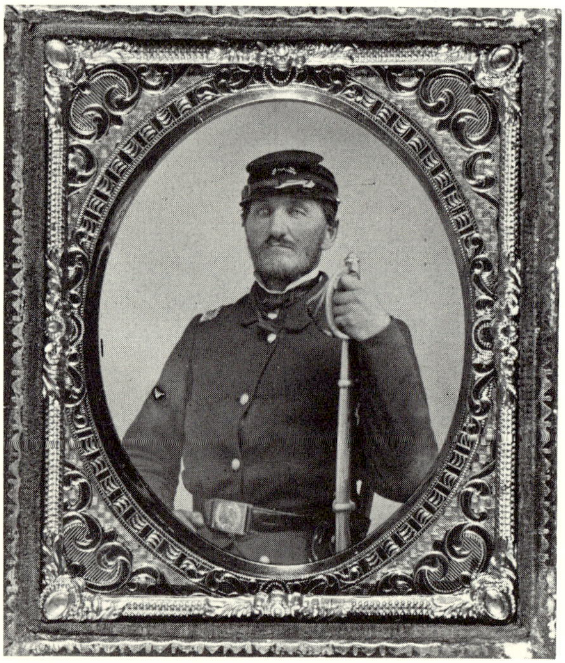

■ *Daguerreotypes* [1839-c. 1857] are generally cased photographs which appear very mirror-like. The tone is usually quite silvery, more like mercury, and they were often hand-tinted. They range in size from 1½ x 1¾ inches (ninth plate) through 8½ x 13 inches (double whole plate). The most commonly found are quarter plate size which are 2¾ x 3¼ inches.

■ *Ambrotypes* [1852-1863] are cased and are often mistaken for daguerreotypes. They do not have the mirror-like appearance, but are generally behind glass. Ambrotypes are simply very underexposed glass negatives placed in front of a black backing of paint, velvet or paper. Hand coloring was often done to make cheeks appear rosy and necklaces appear to be gold.

▣ *Tintypes* [1856-1938] are images made on a metal backing painted black. They work on a principle similar to the ambrotype. Tintypes are extremely durable, but are rarely as lovely to look at as the daguerreotype. The tones are very grayed-over and hand coloring fails to relieve the corpse-like color. Tintypes were produced until the 1930s as a quickie process at carnivals and fairs. They were sometimes cased and glassed to make them appear like the more expensive daguerreotypes and ambrotypes. You may have to take a cased image apart to see whether it is a tintype or an ambrotype. "Chocolate colored" tintypes, introduced in March, 1870, used a dark brown backing which was more flattering to the sitter.

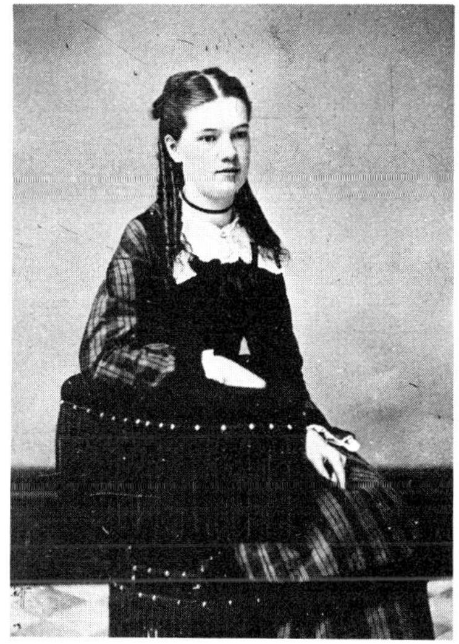

▣ *Cartes-de-Visite* [1859-1914] and *Cabinet Cards* [1866-1914] are mounted on cardboard backings, usually with the name of the studio on the back or in the margin at the bottom of the print. *Cartes-de-visite* (photographic calling cards) were enormously popular and were traded enthusiastically. The print was made on semi-gloss paper mounted on card backings about 2½ x 4 inches. The later *cabinet cards* were introduced to boost the sagging carte-de-visite market. Cabinet cards are similarly put together, but measure 4¼ x 6½ inches. During the Civil War, a tax stamp was required on these photo-

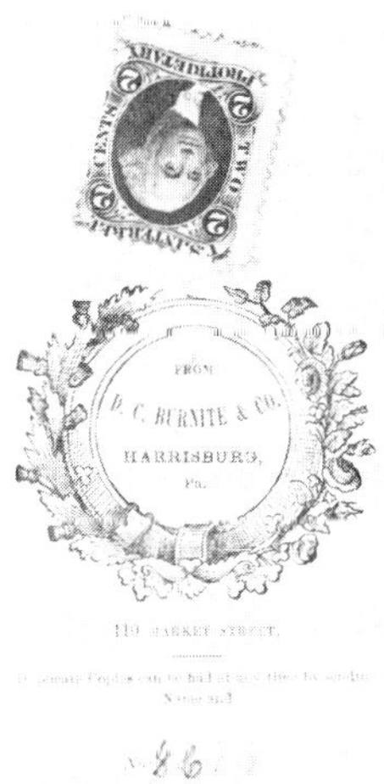

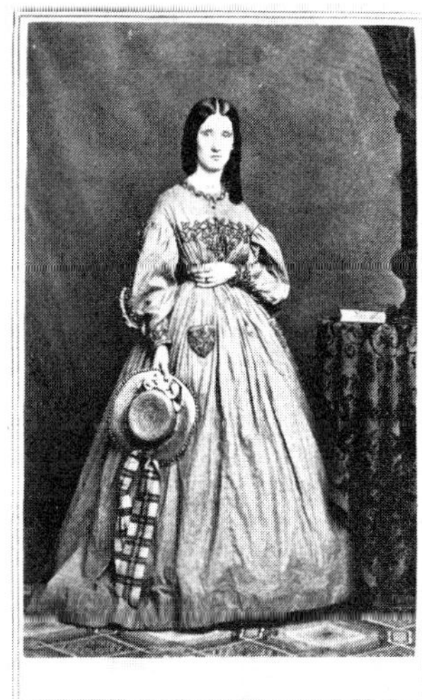

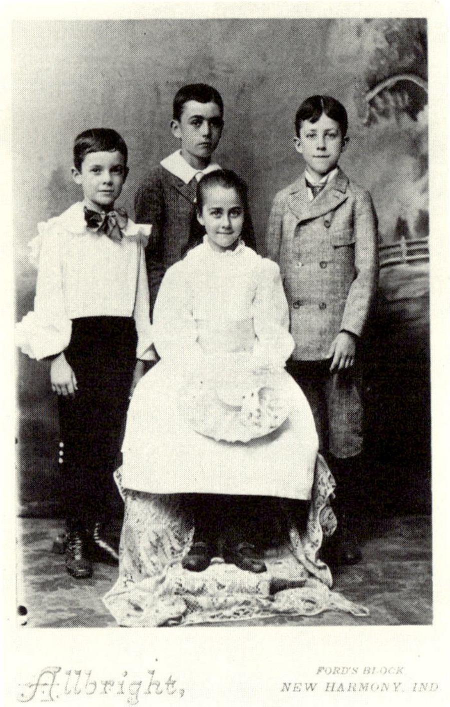

graphs from September 1, 1864 until August 1, 1866. These stamps are usually located on the backs of the cards. Cabinet cards on dark green or maroon stock were probably made in the 1880s.

All of the above were studio-type photographs, with stiffly posed people. The invention of gelatin dry plates made photography feasible for the more casual amateur shooter.

■ Gelatin emulsion on *Glass Negatives* [1878-c. 1930] are, for obvious reasons, delicate. They should be handled with greatest care to avoid dropping and shattering Grandma into smithereens. To be safe, glass negatives should be copied onto modern film.

■ *Flexible Film* became available in 1889. It used a nitrocellulose base which is quite combustible. These should be copied also. Nitrate negatives were replaced by film (as we know it today) in the early 1930s. Many times you can identify the type of film by looking at the film edge. Safety film is the safe replacement for nitrate film. In several of my early safety negatives, the emulsion has separated from the base, ruining them forever. *Copy now!*

■ *Platinum Prints* were popular around the turn of the century and ceased to be made after World War I when platinum became too expensive. These prints have no gloss at all; the image is *in* the paper. Print color ranges from a very cold gray to a warmer sepia color. The tonal range is extraordinary, with very smooth gradations from black to white. *Platinum is the most permanent of all photographic processes.*

■ The *Cyanotype* was invented in 1842 and was used by some photographers until after

1900. The process is an easy one to spot, as prints are a bright blue. It is the same process used to make blueprints. Cyanotypes are inexpensive to make today and are second only to the platinum print in permanence.

■ Among other black and white processes you might also come across are the *Calotype* and *Albumen* paper. The *calotype* [1841-1857] utilized a paper negative and resulted in a paper print with no gloss and a reddish-brown color. The texture of the paper negative is clearly visible. Calotypes are pretty rare. *Albumen paper* used an agg white emulsion which produced a glossy surface and a cold brown print. The image is definitely *on* the surface of the paper, and usually very sharp due to the use of large glass collodion negatives. Albumen paper was in use from 1850 until 1895 when it was replaced by the gelatin papers used today.

Newer processes, too, can help establish dates for photographs. Many color slides and prints have a date stamped on them, making dating them an easy task; but, remember *that the date shown is when the film was processed or when the print was made,* not when the picture was taken.

Process	*Year*
Kodachrome	1935
Kodacolor	1941
Ansco-Color	1942
Ektachrome	1943
Ektacolor	1947
Polaroid	1948
Kodachrome II	1961
Polacolor & Instamatic	1963
SX-70	1973
Kodachrome 25 and Ektachrome 64	1974
Numbers replace names on Kodak film edges	1976

Having found a body of work, you must proceed carefully. All photographic processes are delicate and should be treated as the historical documents they are. You might consider buying some white 'Mickey Mouse' gloves at a camera store. These are simply inexpensive, lint-free cloth gloves that allow you to handle prints and negatives without fear of fingerprint damage. Take your treasure to a clean, dry place with good light, a large table and a comfortable chair or stool.

■ Daguerreotypes are usually in cases so, short of a light dusting, they will not need much care at this point. For dusting use a soft camel's-hair brush which you can find in camera or art supply stores. Tintypes, too, should be dusted off and placed in individual polyethylene bags. Polyethylene (*not* waxed

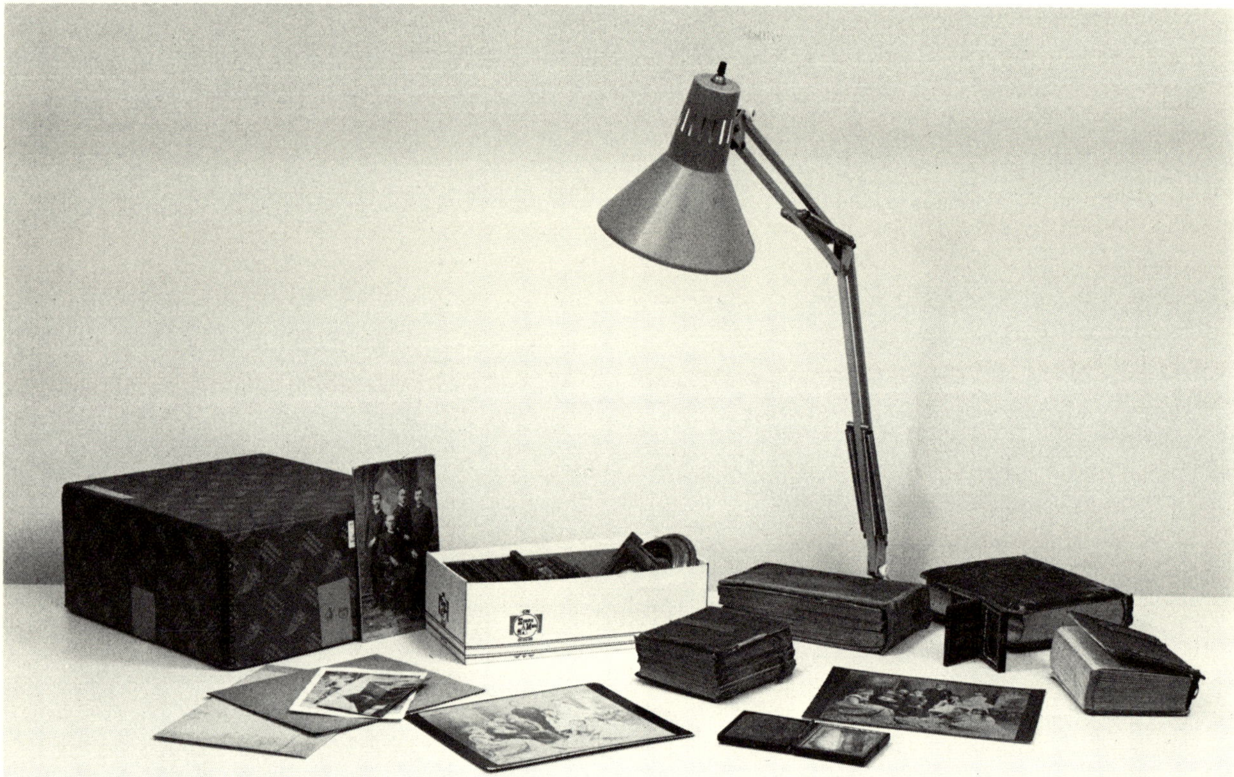

paper) sandwich bags (such as Baggies) can be found in grocery stores. ■ Glass negatives are often found in crumbling brown kraft envelopes. Transfer the negative to a polyethylene bag, but copy any written information from the old envelope onto a piece of good quality writing paper and put it in the bag with the negative. *Never, never write directly on a negative with any kind of writing instrument.* These bits of information may be helpful in dating or placing photographs or perhaps determining who was with whom when. Type or write the information neatly in ink so the person who follows in your footsteps won't have a hard time reading the dates. ■ If negatives are found without envelopes, dust them off before putting them into plastic bags. Dirt is an abrasive and will slowly grind away the image if left unattended. If you have a large number of glass negatives, stack them carefully on edge (in their bags) in a strong poly-foam (*not* foam rubber) lined metal box with a secure bottom. If you find that some of your glass negatives are broken, they may be mended by carefully holding the pieces together with 3M (Scotch) #850 acrylic tape. Place a thin strip of the tape along the edge that the crack passes through. *Tape only the glass side of the negative;* applying tape to the emulsion side might lift off the emulsion, ruining the negative. Support the damaged negative on a piece of clean glass and make a copy negative as soon as possible. Avoid excessive handling of the negatives to prevent chipping the emulsion along the cracked edge. Properly done, a good copy negative will show little evidence of the crack. ■ *Roll film* is often found tightly rolled up, sometimes with a rubber band around it. Remove and discard the rubber band and unroll the film only far enough to identify it. After that, leave it rolled (you won't need the rubber band) until you do whatever printing or copy work you have planned. Old film, especially nitrate, may be extremely brittle. Store newer, still-flexible negatives in strips, flat, in polyethylene negative preservers. *The less you handle negatives, the better off they will be.* Prints should be dusted off with a camel's-hair brush. If they are curled up in little tubes, leave them that way until you begin your restoration effort. In the meantime, place them loosely in a clean box to avoid crushing and creasing them. ■ In among the photographs you will almost certainly find written or printed documents such as newspaper clippings and letters. They are often extremely fragile, but will add invaluable information to the photographs. Newspaper stock (newsprint) is full of acid and becomes crumbly very fast. Always handle paper documents gently. Support them with a piece of clean mat board to avoid tearing when you carry them. Probably the best thing to do is to have the documents copied on a Xerox machine or other copier that uses cotton fiber paper. Such paper is more neutral chemically and will not disintegrate after a few years. Be sure that the copier is *not* the kind that runs the original through the machine; your document would almost certainly be eaten. After being copied, the originals can be plastic heat-laminated in order to preserve them. Store copies of letters and documents in a print box by themselves to prevent possible contamination of photographic prints. ■ Your entire family – as many people as you can think of – should be advised of your project. If they are within travelling distance, you might host an afternoon of going through photographs playing 'who's that?' Undoubtedly the day will be full of stories. A tape recorder can capture these reminiscences easily. Many people are reluctant to 'perform' for a recording machine. If you explain the importance of their stories, how necessary they are to making the pictures come alive, your family may be more willing to forget about the recorder and to enjoy themselves. ■ Relatives reachable only by mail should be sent *numbered* copy prints. Ask them to sit down with the prints and to give you all of the information they can about each photograph by number. Here again, the cassette tape recorder is an excellent way to keep people from skimping on their information. It is more spontaneous and much easier to talk than it is to type or write. Your relatives should be asked the newsman's four W's: Who, What, Where and When? Be sure they identify which picture they are talking about by mentioning the number you have written on the back of the print. You, of course, have a duplicate set of prints to identify which stories go with which prints. When all of the information is received, it will be your job to transcribe it on to good quality paper. When writing on the backs of prints, use a soft lead pencil. Place the print face down on a piece of clean glass and write only on the outside edges of the print's back. *Never use ballpoint or felt-tip pens on photographs and never, never write directly on the face of the print.* ■ People whose portraits are on daguerreotypes are all dead. If you can't identify a person in a daguerreotype, you probably never will. Most cabinet card people are dead, too, but some people still living may remember who they were. Identify your collection now, before the people in your Kodachromes start to go. ■ At this point you should have standing all about you your family's photographic heritage. Treat it gently, no smoking or coffee cups anywhere nearby. One mishap could destroy images that have survived a century. The next step is to restore the images for your enjoyment and to preserve them for future generations.

Burbank, Cal., Feby 11, 1916.

Master George C. Davies, D.L.
4510 Chester Ave.,
Philadelphia, Pa.

My Dear Boy:—

I was very glad to receive your last letter and to learn about the train. I hope it will continue to run all right and be a source of much pleasure to you.

I did feel the need of a deputy legs yesterday. Your grandmother got rabbit hungry, and I had to walk away up to Mr. Prater's to buy a rabbit. I got a very nice, big young one. It weighed 3½ pounds, in a sack, alive.

II
Restoration of the Photographs

Over the years, through handling by generations of hands, photographs become damaged. In this chapter we will describe methods of restoring images to something near their original condition. This can be risky, however, and you should be certain beforehand that restoration will markedly improve the image. Consider that at this point the image may be lost forever, and determine whether the condition of the image can only be improved by restoration attempts. *Before doing any restoration work, you should make a copy photograph as a safety precaution.* If something nasty should happen, you will at least have an acceptable record of the photograph. As you may surmise from the above, restoration is a serious thing and should not be entered into lightly. ▣ *Copying* is a necessary skill for the family photo-historian. By copying, you can make modern, archival negatives and prints from fading and fragile originals. Prints held with rubber cement in photo albums will almost certainly become stained. Color snapshots, too, should be copied to ensure their images lasting for future generations. You should be aware that *color as we know it today begins fading in about 20 years.* ▣ Copy equipment can be as simple or as complex as your taste and pocketbook permit. If you would like to afford a good copy setup, but can't, perhaps you can interest a local organization in sponsoring one. Church groups, historical societies, camera clubs, libraries and fraternal organizations could collect enough money from interested members to buy a first-rate outfit. A community darkroom can be established in the same way to provide archival processing and printing facilities. ▣ Instamatic cameras fitted with accessory closeup lenses will do an adequate copying job using Verichrome Pan black and white film. With these cameras, however, there is the problem called parallax. That is, the lens and the viewfinder, because of their separate locations, see different views. The most popular form of parallax error is the famous cut-off head trick wherein the viewfinder, being higher, sees the subject's head, but the lens, down below, has a more abdominal perspective. The problem becomes acute in closeup work. So always be certain, by measuring if necessary, that the lens is seeing the work properly. ▣ 35mm cameras, particularly the single lens reflex types with through-the-lens meters, are excellent for copying photographs. Most of these cameras will focus to 18 inches and even closer with accessories. I would recommend using extension tubes or bellows attachments over closeup lenses. Tubes and bellows simply move the lens farther from the film, allowing for closer focus. Auxiliary closeup lenses, which mount on the front of the normal lens, tend to be

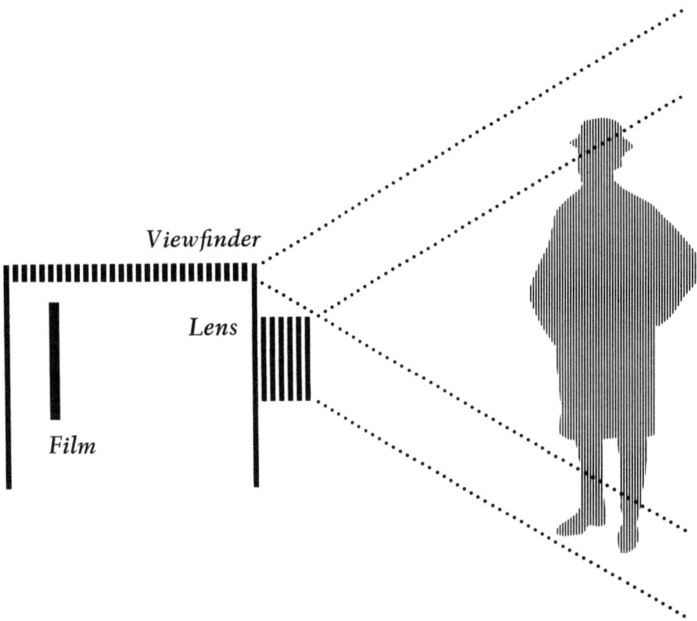

unsharp. If you find you are going to be doing a lot of copy work and can afford it, I highly recommend a macro lens. Such a lens focuses to a 1 : 1 reproduction ratio; in other words, the image on the negative is the same size as the original. Macro lenses are, as a rule, extremely sharp and will give fine results. A recommended 35mm film is Kodak's Panatomic-X. ■ Cameras using 120 size roll film can give very good results. Twin lens reflexes such as the Rolleiflex, Mamiyaflex or Yashicamat are tricky to use because of the parallax problem. If you are careful to raise the camera the precise distance which separates the viewing and taking lenses before you make the exposure, you'll have no problems. Of the three cameras, the Mamiyaflex is capable of closeup work without accessories. The other two are limited to using closeup lenses. Roll film single lens reflex cameras, pricey jewels that they are, are excellent for copy work. ■ Press cameras and view cameras, using large sheet film (up to 8 x 10 inches) can occasionally be found in out-of-the-way pawn shops for a reasonable sum. I found my first view camera in a hospital thrift shop for $25 with lens and film holders. These are bulky cameras, but they will give you the best reproduction quality possible. In addition, various types of film useful in copy work (such as Kodak's excellent Professional Copy Film) are made only in sheet film sizes. ■ A relatively new product which should be of great value to the home copyist is Polaroid's Type 665 Positive/Negative film. Using 665 in a conventional Polaroid camera with closeup attachments will instantly yield both a positive *and* a usable negative 3¼ x 4¼ inches in size. The coated print and the properly treated negative can be considered archival. The film is not cheap, but you are paying not only for the material itself, but also for the speed and convenience of the instant process. Adaptor backs are available which will allow you to use 665 in a 4 x 5 press or view camera. ■ Both black and white and color prints should be as clean as possible before you make your copies. Pencil marks can be gently erased with a gum eraser. Dirt, grease and other blotches from the past should be removed with Kodak film cleaner applied with a cotton swab or a cotton ball. Fungus growths, which find the gelatin coating on photographs tasty, can be removed in the same way. Be certain to change the cotton often in order to prevent spreading spores. Fungus thrives in humid conditions; proper storage will prevent their return. ■ Photographic prints often seem to surpass the Dead Sea Scrolls in their resistance to flattening efforts. By moistening the back of the print with a damp-dry cotton ball and weighting with books until dry, the print will regain some flatness.

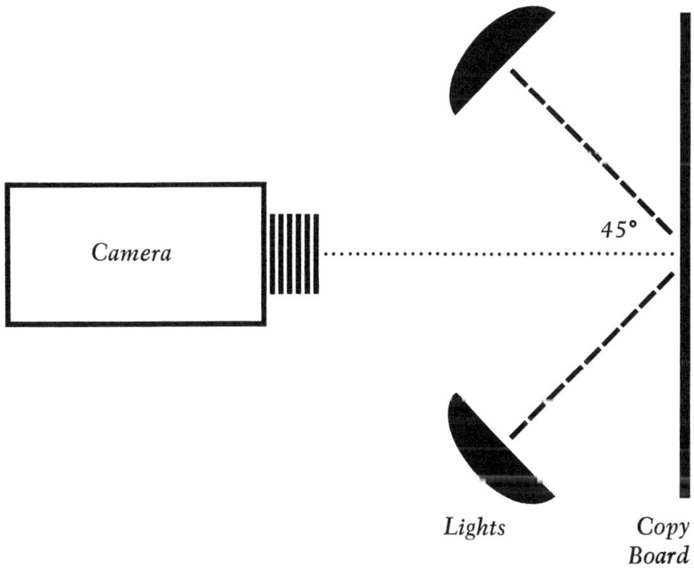

In extreme cases, the entire print can be soaked in a tray of distilled water until the paper relaxes. It can then be dried on a fiber-glass screen (see Chapter III). ■ To make good copies, you will need some method of holding the camera steadily and squarely in front of the original photo. Most anything will work, from a stack of books to a super expensive copy stand. Between the extremes there are suitable alternatives such as moderately priced tripods and home-made wooden copy stands. The only thing more expensive copy equipment will do is make the operation a bit smoother. ■ Lights should be set up at 45 degree angles to the copy work (see diagram). These can be household lamps, but reflector floods will put out more light, making for shorter exposures. The camera back should be parallel to the original in both horizontal and vertical planes. ■ Instructions packed with closeup lenses and other copying equipment should be followed exactly to achieve greatest clarity in the copy photograph. ■ In copying tintypes (which are usually dented and scratched) and modern 'silk finished' prints, reflections from the surface present annoying problems. A piece of polarized plastic placed over each light source will cut reflections if a third piece of similar plastic is placed over the camera lens. The piece on the camera lens must be rotated until the maximum glare-cutting effect is achieved. ■ Faded yellow or reddish-brown photographs may be copied through a blue filter (Kodak Wratten #47B) to enhance the contrast in the copy.* In general, filters lighten similar colors and darken opposite colors. ■ Determine exposure by reading a Kodak 18% gray card with your light meter. This will give you proper exposure for your lighting conditions without regard for the brightness of the original. There are, however, several exposure problems that may crop up. In using filters, you will have to increase the exposure to compensate for the amount of light the filter is absorbing. Cameras with behind-the-lens meters compensate for this automatically. Because different filters block different amounts of light, you will have to follow Table A to determine proper exposure if you are using a hand-held meter. For example, to get a proper exposure with a Kodak Wratten #12 (yellow) filter, you must increase the indicated exposure by 1 f/stop, from say, ½ second @ f/11 to ½ second @ f/8. With exposure times longer than one second, you must increase exposure to get proper exposure. This circular bit of information is called reciprocity departure. To correct for this, it is best to increase the aperture (f/stop), because lengthening the exposure time only compounds the problem – similar to chasing one's tail.

Filter Factors for Panchromatic Film

Kodak Wratten #	*Color*	*Increase f/stops*
6 (K1)	Light Yellow	½
8 (K2)	Yellow	1
12	Yellow	1
15G	Yellow/Orange	1½
23A	Red/Orange	2
25A	Red	3
29F	Dark Red	4
47B	Blue	2½
58B	Green	3
11 (X1)	Green	2
13 (X2)	Green	2½
C5	Blue	2½
Polarizer	Gray	1-3

Reciprocity Correction

Indicated Exposure Time	*Increase f/stops*
1 second	⅓
5 seconds	⅔
15 seconds	1
45 seconds	1⅓
2 minutes	1⅔
5 minutes	2
10 minutes	2⅓
20 minutes	2⅔
40 minutes	3

**In these descriptions, I recommend Kodak products for two reasons: first, I have used them and they work; second, like Fords and Chevys, they are available through dealers just about everywhere.*

For example, if your light meter indicates an exposure of 15 seconds at f/22, proper exposure would be 15 seconds at f/16. ■ The third problem is met only when you are using a view camera, or accessory bellows or extension tubes on a smaller camera. The theory behind this one – called bellows factor – is that the farther the lens is moved from the film (the closer the subject), the smaller the effective aperture (f/stop). A table cannot be given for this, because each different focal length lens has different bellows factors. There is a formula by which you can calculate your bellow:

$$\text{F/stop to be set for proper exposure} = \frac{\text{F/stop indicated by meter x lens' focal length}}{\text{Bellows extension}}$$

The problem is more easily solved with a little book called the Kodak Master Photoguide In the back is a handy dial (the thing is up to its ears in handy dials) which will figure your bellows factors for you. ■ If you have a combination of the above to contend with, e.g., 2 stops worth of bellows, 1⅓ stops of reciprocity and 2 stops of filter factor, these increases should be *added* together to make an increase of 5⅓ stops over the indicated exposure. ■ If you don't have a light meter, either hand-held or built into your camera, read the directions that come with the film. They will give you a starting exposure. Keep a record of your exposures so that when you see the results, you will know what you did right and what you did wrong. Always have the conditions as much the same as possible, with lights the same distance from the copy material and so on. ■ If you have copied a badly scratched original, your copy print can be greatly improved with application of spotting colors. Spotone is recommended for this step. It takes a certain amount of skill and a very fine 000 red sable brush, but Spotone will make a scratched print look almost as good as new. Follow the directions packed with the colors (the manufacturer knows whereof he speaks) and keep the brush just barely dampened with the spotting color. A drop of Photo-Flo in the diluting water prevents the color from beading up when it is applied. By all means, practice on reject prints before you begin spotting in earnest. Spotting original prints can be dangerous. Cracks in the print emulsion drink up Spotone with little color change, and if you blow it on the original you are stuck. Spot the copy print, you'll be safer that way. ■ Glass, nitrocellulose and color negatives should be copied onto modern film. The easiest material to use is Kodak's Professional Direct Duplicating Film (SO-015) available on special order from any Kodak dealer. It comes in sheet form only, in sizes from 4 x 5 to 11 x 14 inches. Negatives can be either contact printed or enlarged on to SO-015 to yield excellent negatives in many ways better than the originals. The film is developed in trays in total darkness using Dektol developer. The whole process takes only about 5 minutes. If your negatives are badly scratched on the shiny side, a light application of Edwal No-Scratch or petroleum jelly to that side will magically make scratches disappear from subsequent prints. ■ Color slides may be copied onto black and white film using a bellows slide copying attachment on a 35mm single lens reflex. You will be fighting increased contrast every inch of the way, so you should develop your film (Pan-X) about 30% less than the recommended time. If you have an enlarger, color slides may be enlarged onto Professional Copy Film and can be cropped, burned in and dodged in the process.

■ *Ambrotypes* are very easily restored. An ambrotype is nothing more than a glass negative held in front of a black backing by a brass frame, with the image, out of its case. Pry or paint; it is usually this which needs restoration. With an X-acto knife, pry the brass frame, with the image, out of its case. Pry carefully from all sides. When it is free, gently bend the frame and remove the ambrotype, cover glass and backing. Sometimes paper tape holds the ambrotype together. The glue is usually so dry the tape will fall off; but in stubborn cases, slit the tape with the knife to separate the contents.

Thick	cover glass	brass frame
Thin	brass mat	
Medium	ambrotype negative	
Thinnest	black backing	

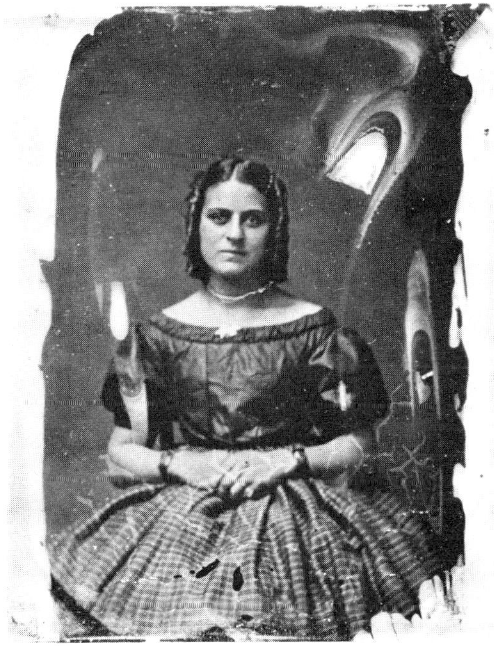

If the backing is painted on the glass negative, it will have to be scraped off with a razor blade. Before you begin to scrape, make doubly sure that it is the backing you are scraping and not the negative emulsion. Black paper and cloth backings can be removed from the negative easily. ■ After the backing has been removed, clean both sides of the cover glass and the surface of the negative that does not have the emulsion (the negative image) on it. Use a soft cloth *dampened* with soapy distilled water. Be sure

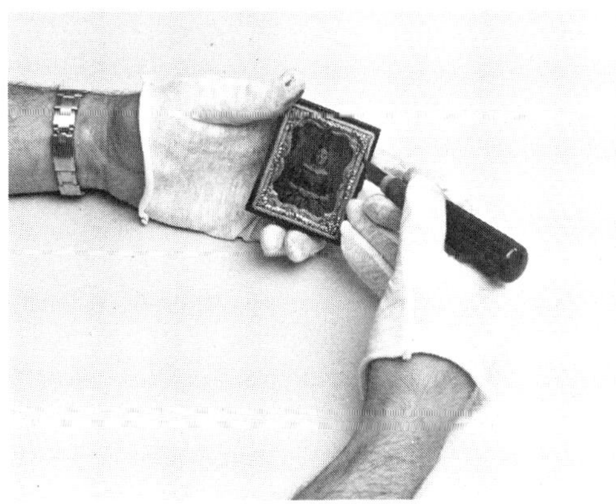

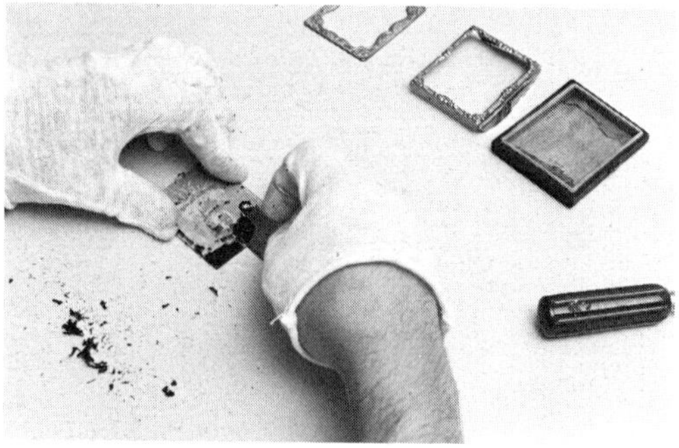

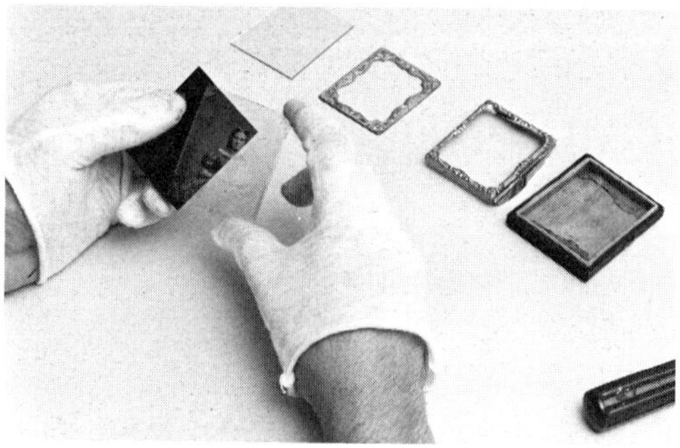

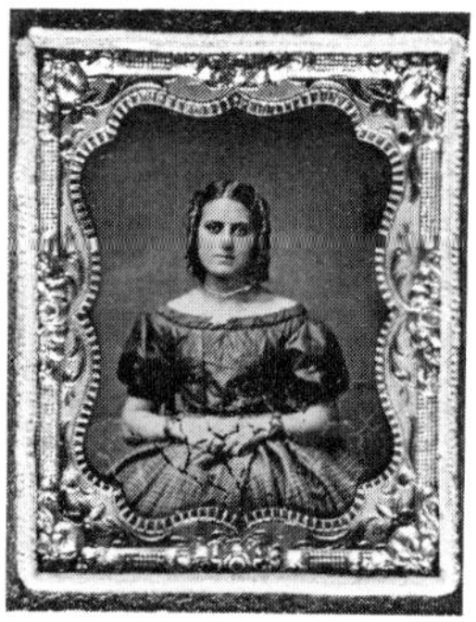

you don't get any moisture on the emulsion side. ■ A new backing can be made from black paper, black velvet, or black plastic cut from a trash bag. Ilford photographic paper comes in a black plastic bag that is a nice, rich black, perfect for backing ambrotypes. Once the surfaces are cleaned and the new backing is made, reassemble the pieces and wrap the brass frame around them. Be sure the frame is tight. If it is too loosely wrapped, you may split the case when the frame and its contents are replaced. Make another copy now that the ambrotype looks better.

■ *Daguerreotypes.* Like fancy chefs, early daguerreotypists practiced their craft using a pinch of this and a dash of that. As a result, different daguerreotypes respond in different ways to restoration efforts. ■ A good copy should be made before restoration is attempted because in rare instances the image may disappear completely. Proceed with caution and attempt restoration only on daguerreotypes that are heavily tarnished. The image is formed by a combination of mercury and silver on a silver-plated copper sheet. It is, in the words of one of Daguerre's contemporaries, "as delicate as a butterfly's wing." Be careful; the image scratches very easily. ■ The first method of removing tarnish requires a bit of hunting for chemicals. Most can be found in chemical supply houses, but you might also check with your local college chemistry department. You will need:

Distilled water
Mild soap (not detergent)
Thiourea
85% Phosphoric acid
95% Grain alcohol
Kodak Photo-Flo
Several 8 x 10″ print trays
Rubber gloves
Hair dryer
Cotton gloves

Remove the daguerreotype from its case and disassemble. It is taken apart in the same manner as an ambrotype. White cotton gloves will keep fingerprints at a safe distance, but even so, *handle these images only by the edges.* ▣ Clean the cover glass in a solution of distilled water and mild soap, then rinse and dry thoroughly. (You have of course, by this time, removed your white cotton gloves.) ▣ The daguerreotype is then sloshed gently in the soap and water solution to remove any remaining tape and the grime of ages. Again, hold the daguerreotype plate only by the edges and do not touch or rub the image. Rinse in clear distilled water. Now, using rubber gloves, dip the daguerreotype plate into a tray containing the following solution:

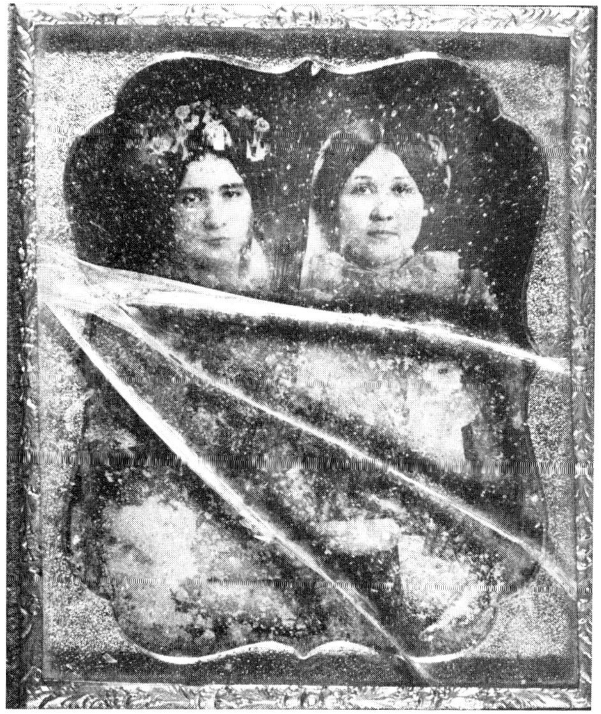

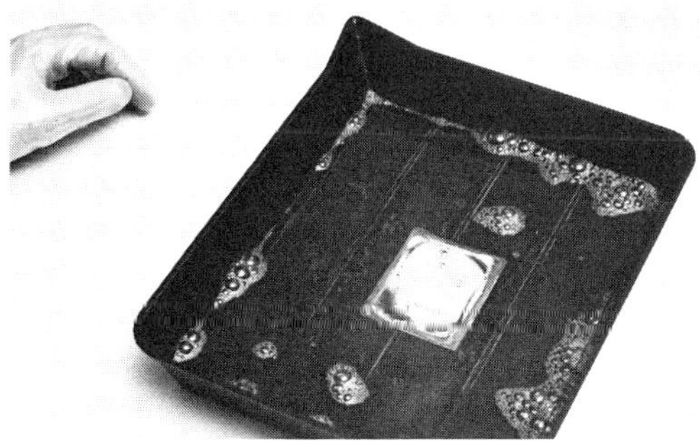

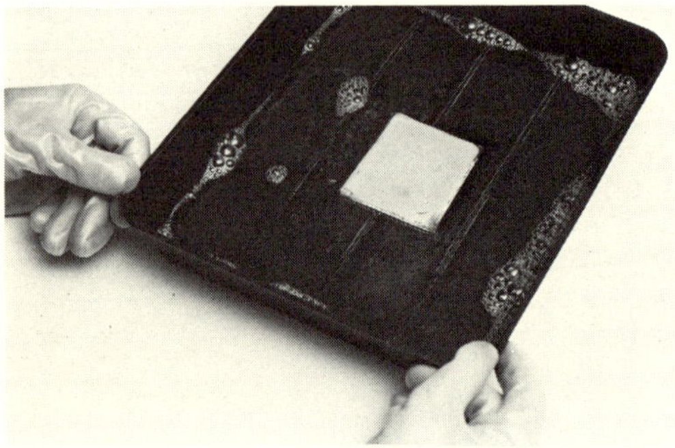

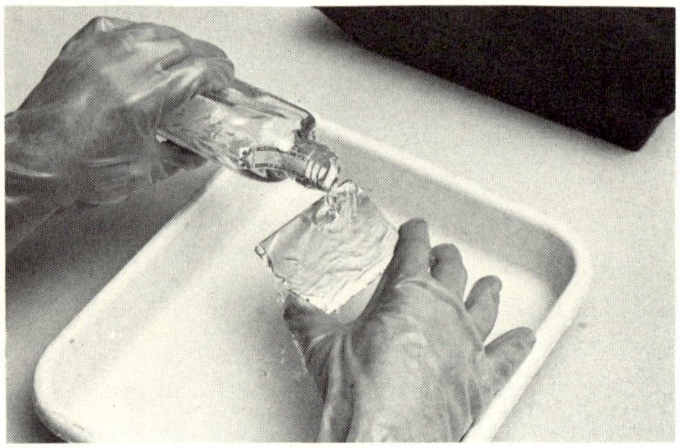

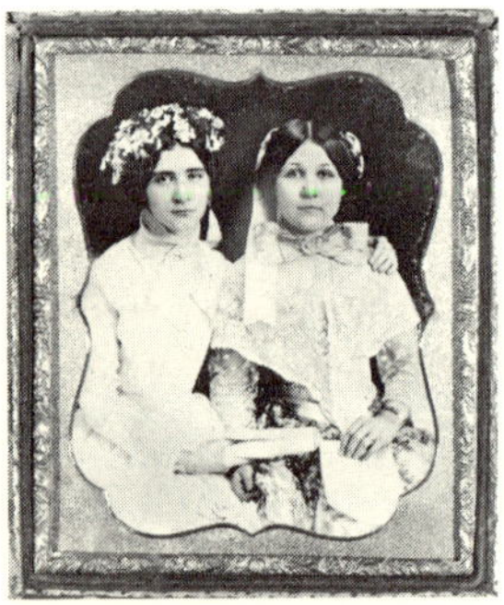

In 16 ounces of distilled water, dissolve
2⅓ ounces Thiourea
¼ ounce 85% Phosphoric acid
1 drop Photo-Flo
Add sufficient water to make 32 ounces of solution.

Thiourea can be measured on a small postage scale using a paper cup to hold the powder. Be certain you have adjusted the scale to compensate for the weight of the cup and discard the cup immediately after use. Slosh the daguerreotype in the thiourea solution face up by gently rocking the tray. The tarnished areas should clear up quickly. Rinse the plate in two changes of distilled water and then dry it by pouring 95% grain alcohol over both sides and draining completely. Play an electric hair dryer set on low heat over both the front and back of the plate. Slipping back into your white gloves, reassemble the daguerreotype. ▣ An alternative to the above method uses readily available tarnish removing silver dip. Follow the instructions as outlined, but substitute silver dip such as Instant Dip or Goddard's Silver Dip for the thiourea/phosphoric acid solution. The remainder of the process is the same. ▣

Never use a silver polish on daguerreotype plates! You will surely rub the image right into oblivion.

▣ *Printing-out Processes.* If you have in your family collection a number of glass plate negatives, you might want to make prints using either one of the two following processes. Neither one requires a darkroom. ▣ Glass negatives were much more contrasty than modern films. When you try to print glass negatives on modern printing paper, the resulting images look like so much soot and chalk. The highlights, especially, look washed out. Printing-out processes are so-called because the image is formed during exposure to light rather than during development as with conventional materials. When the image prints, the shadow areas of the print darken first. As this happens, the filtering effect of the darkened emulsion prevents it from darkening further. The highlights, meanwhile remaining relatively light, continue to get the full effect of the exposing light. The result of this 'self-masking' effect is a normal contrast print from an extremely contrasty negative. ▣ The first process uses Kodak Studio Proof paper and sodium thiosulphate. Studio Proof, printing-out paper (or P.O.P. for short) is used by studio photographers for portrait proofs. Normally, it is left unfixed, so it will slowly fade on exposure to light. It can be fixed, however, and the image color is a lovely horse-chestnut brown. Sodium thiosulphate is a fixer. Most prepared fixers contain a hardening agent

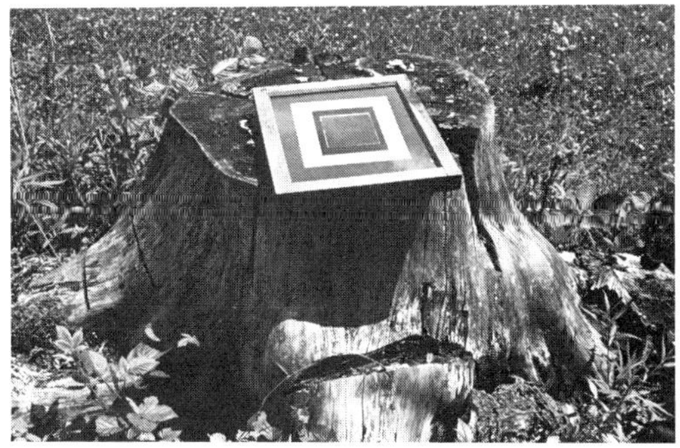

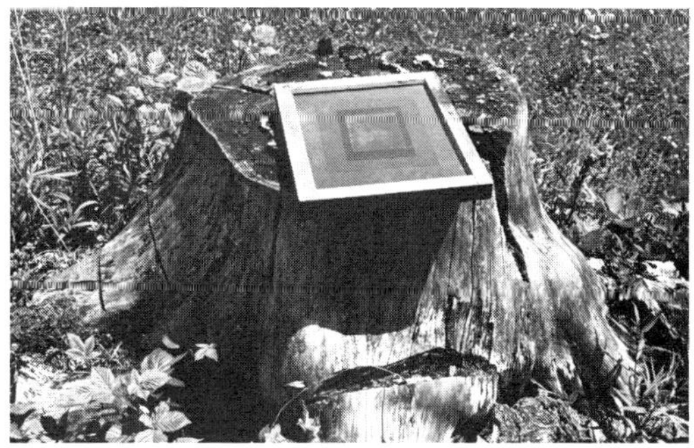

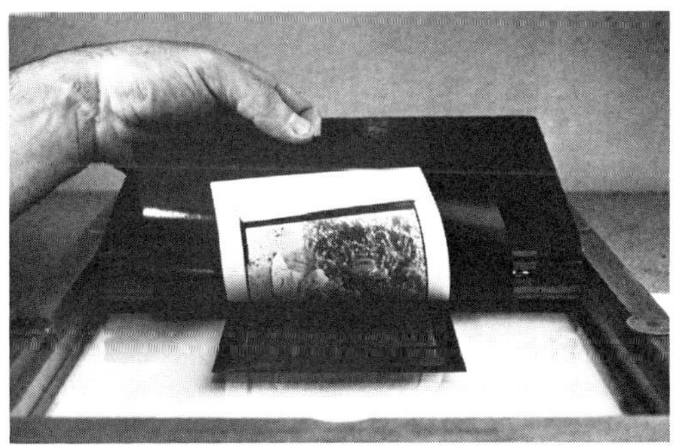

which turns P.O.P. an ugly yellow. Thiosulphate contains no hardeners, hence horse-chestnut brown shades will appear. To make things easier you will need a printing frame with a split, hinged back. Antique stores and flea markets sometimes have these, or, you can buy them new from Photo Materials Corp. (see appendix), a manufacturer of photographic paraphernalia. Another type, the Premier print frame, is available at many photo stores. ■ First, clean the negative. Brush dust from the emulsion (dull) side with a soft camel's-hair brush. Clean the glass (shiny) side with a cloth dampened with soapy distilled water, being careful not to get moisture on the emulsion. If you do, allow the negative to air dry by leaning it, emulsion side up, against a vertical surface, such as a short stack of books. ■ Place the negative emulsion-side up in the printing frame. A sheet of Studio Proof paper (which can be handled in dim room light) is then placed shiny side down on top of the negative. Close the printing frame and place it outside on a table, bench or tree stump in direct sunlight. Exposure time will range from two minutes to several hours depending on the latitude, the season, the weather, the time of day and the density of the negative. Check the exposure by finding a shady spot, opening one-half of the frame and lifting the P.O.P. away from the negative. Darkest shadow areas should be olive green with an almost metallic appearance. It will look much too dark overall; but don't worry. (The next step is to trundle it to a dimly lit room where we will make it right.) Replace the loose half of the printing frame for the journey to the dimly lit room to prevent the paper from fogging. ■ In the oft-mentioned dimly lit room, prepare a solution of 32 ounces of tap water and 5 heaping tablespoons of sodium thiosulphate. The thiosulphate, which looks like rock salt, must be thoroughly dissolved and the solution must be 70 degrees or cooler. A warmer solution would wash the emulsion off. Place the print in a tray containing the thiosulphate solution, flip it over a few times, then rock the tray for five minutes with the print face up. Be sure the solution is covering the face of the print as you rock. ■ When the five-minute period is over, repeat the process for a second five minutes, using a fresh fixing bath prepared in the same way. The print will lighten considerably in the fixing baths and take on a pleasing color. Each quart of fixer is good for only one 8 x 10 inch print. When the time is up, wash the print in ten changes of water at 70 degrees. Flip the print over several times in each change of water. Drain the print and place it in a tray containing a hypo clearing bath such as Kodak's Hypo Clearing Agent or Heico Perma Wash.

Perma Wash is recommended because it is a liquid concentrate, much easier to handle than Kodak's powder. Agitate the print in this solution for five minutes, drain, and return to a clean tray where it is rinsed in another ten changes of water, with agitation. Hang the print to dry by clipping a suspended clothespin to one corner. The emulsion on P.O.P. is extremely soft, and drying by any other method would risk damage to the image. ▣ When dry, the print will be curly. Flatten it by rubbing a damp-dry cotton ball over the back of the print and weighting down with books. An alternate method employs an electric iron with all of its steam water removed. Set the iron for 'wool' and iron two pieces of clean, acid-free mat board until the moisture is driven from them. Place the print, dry and face up, between the pieces of board and iron the entire surface for about a minute. Upon removal, the print will be smooth and flat.

▣ *Note: Choose a work surface for ironing carefully!* Finished wooden surfaces will suffer damage if subjected to heat from an iron. An ironing board or Formica counter top will work very well if protected by a ½ inch piece of homosote or several pieces of thick, non-corrugated cardboard. ▣ If you find that you are making a lot of prints, you can prepare a stock solution of fixer which will make your results much more consistent. To make a gallon of stock fixer, dissolve 5 cups of sodium thiosulphate crystals in a half gallon of hot water. Add sufficient warm water after adding the crystals to make 1 gallon of fixer stock. Let it cool. For use, add 16 ounces of stock solution to 16 ounces of cold water. Be sure the solution is 70 degrees or cooler. Kodak Rapid Fix can also be used to fix P.O.P. It comes in two bottles, the fixer and a separate hardener. Dilute the Rapid Fix solution A following the directions for paper, and eliminate the hardener, part B. Fixing time is three minutes for each bath. Printing-out paper is an extremely easy and inexpensive way to make beautiful prints from early negatives. Indeed, children can be taught the basics of the negative/positive process quite easily using Studio Proof paper and thiosulphate.

▣ In Chapter I we mentioned the *cyanotype or blueprint process*. It is one of the earliest photographic processes and is quite easy to do. You will need some good quality writing paper, such as Crane's Kid Finish or a smooth watercolor paper. I have used Fabriano 92 lb. plate finish drawing paper (available at art supply stores) with excellent results. Its surface works well with negatives having fine detail. You will also need two chemicals – potassium ferricyanide and ferric ammonium

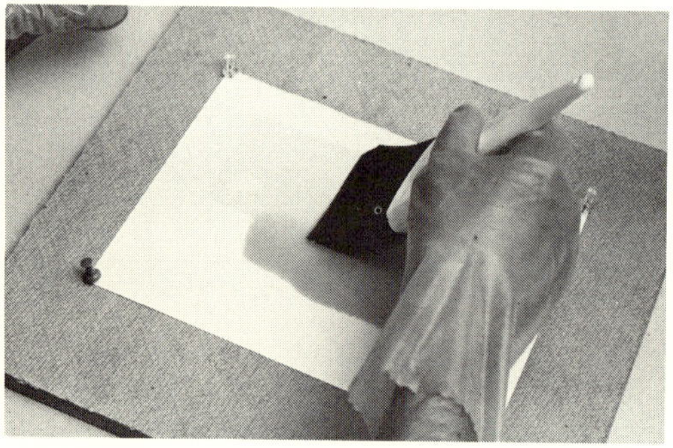

citrate. Kodak sells ferricyanide, but you'll have to get the ferric ammonium citrate from a chemical supply house. You'll also need some distilled water.

Part A: In 8 ounces distilled water, dissolve 2 ounces ferric ammonium citrate.

Part B: In 8 ounces distilled water, dissolve 1½ ounces potassium ferricyanide.

To use: mix equal parts of A and B. For an 8 x 10 inch negative, print on a piece of paper at least 8½ x 11 inches and use 5 cc's of each chemical. Pour the combined solutions onto the center of the paper which has been secured to a piece of cardboard with pushpins. Spread the solution with a polyfoam brush. Available in hardware stores, these brushes are cheap and spread the liquid evenly. Brush first up and down and then across the page until there is no streaking. If the streaks are hard to eliminate, shake out the brush and work on the paper again, up and down, side to side. The streaking should disappear. ■ Hang the paper to dry (or dry with a hair dryer) in a darkened room. If you are doing more than one print, coat and dry the others at this time. You should, however, coat only as many as you'll do that day; coated, unexposed cyanotype paper stores poorly. ■ When you are certain that the paper is dry, contact print in the same manner as described for the printing-out paper. Expose until the shadow areas are a charcoal blue, almost gray. Wash the exposed print in several changes of plain tap water, giving enough soaking time in each bath to allow the yellow in the highlights to clear to white. When the discarded water runs clear, without any trace of yellow, hang the print to dry, clipping one corner to a suspended clothespin. No need for a darkened room during drying. Because the light-sensitive chemicals are in the paper and not coated on the surface as with P.O.P., you'll have no trouble with curly cyanotypes. Cyanotypes are second only to platinum in permanence, and will last as long as the paper they are printed on.

■ *Platinum printing* is a third process which you may want to investigate. It is more expensive than the other two, but it is capable of beautiful, delicate prints of unsurpassed permanence. Heretofore, platinum was sold only in large quantities, making it extremely expensive for the small-time user. A company in Wilmington, Delaware, Elegant Images (see Appendix B), now packages platinum materials in quantities small enough to be afforded by the amateur. Their instructions and trouble-shooting guide are clearly written, and they are constantly researching to improve their products. A book entitled *Caring For Photographs* (published by Time-Life Books) has an excellent chapter describing the platinum process in detail. It is still an expensive process no matter how you slice it, but for a few key images in your collection, platinum would work beautifully. ▣ *All of these processes are by necessity contact printing processes;* that is, you cannot get a print larger than the negative size. But there is another printing-out process that allows you to enlarge contrasty negatives to any print size you want. It uses conventional printing paper and requires a darkroom setup. ▣ Under safelight illumination, develop an *unexposed* piece of #5 or #6 contrast grade printing paper in regular paper developer for two minutes with constant agitation. Drain the paper and hang it by a corner in a totally darkened room. When the print is tacky-damp, place it in the easel and enlarge it in the normal way; the only difference is that the enlarger light is left on. As you watch, amazing things happen. The print image, appearing first as a negative, soon seems to flex and writhe. After a few seconds of this the image disappears, the positive print cancelling out the negative image. The image prints out because the developer is already in the paper. The self-masking effect takes place, yielding a very soft, un-contrasty print from an impossibly contrasty negative. Exposure time is determined by turning off the enlarger light whereupon you will see a positive print. Keep exposing until the desired darkness is achieved. If the print looks OK in the highlights, but the shadows are weak, a quick dip in the developer will darken them to an acceptable level. When it has sufficiently cooked, stop, fix and wash according to Chapter III. ▣ This fascinating bit was found in David Vestal's excellent and very readable book, *The Craft of Photography* (Harper & Row). It should be everyone's first technical book.

III

In the Daylight Darkroom: Archival Processes

The family photo-historian should realize that all labors will be for nought if the photographs fade away. Color in any form, as it now stands, cannot hold a candle to black and white in terms of permanence. Indeed, *the only way we can preserve color images is by copying them with black and white film.* ▣ Commercial photo labs – from the fanciest, most professional to the local drugstore – rarely give two hoots about permanence. You might even consider yourself lucky to receive your negatives without scratches or fingerprints. No one, anywhere, should or will care as much about your negatives as you do. When you make photographs for the future, process them yourself and be certain of their permanence. The setup for processing is not expensive and excellent results can be had in a full-time bathroom. ▣ All modern black and white films are capable of beautiful, full-toned, almost grainless results. Careful processing will ensure that these qualities are not lost. Any introductory photo book will give you the essentials of film processing, but there are a few techniques that are not well known that I have used with success in relatively primitive conditions.

(1) The processing tank to use is a Patterson System 4. Don't let anyone talk you into anything else. I used steel tanks for ten years and switched to Patterson plastic tanks only after

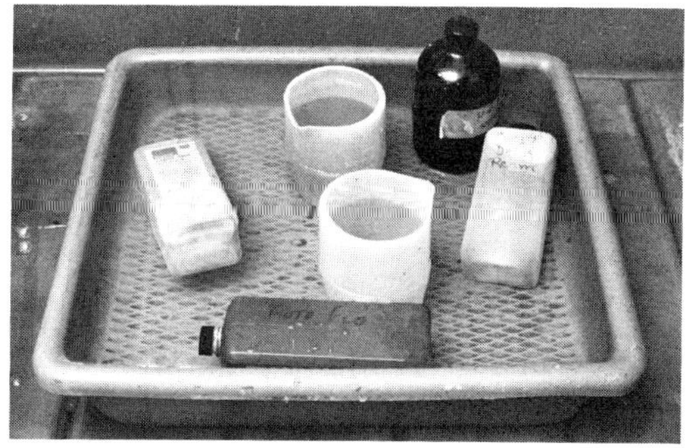

seeing that they are capable of much more even development. *Read the instruction book for best results.*

Sheet film is best developed in trays; you increase the chances for streaking when you use film hangers.

(2) All of the chemicals in their respective bottles should be placed in a common container such as a big tray or bathtub. (I use a blue plastic tray that measures 20 x 22 x 5 inches. It was found in a swimming pool supply store.) With the tray filled with water, all of the chemicals will, after about an hour, come to one temperature. *Consistency of temperature is vital to good processing.* For washing and rinsing the film, use water from the tray; water from a faucet may vary by as much as 20 degrees causing irreparable damage to the film.

(3) Before pouring developer into the tank,

pre-soak the film for one minute, using water from the tray with constant agitation. The pre-soak eliminates air bubbles on the film which appear as black spots on prints.

(4) Use a one-shot developer such as D-76 diluted 1 : 1 and discard it after use. More consistent results are achieved by not using a potentially exhausted developer.

(5) Use only the proper dilution of stop bath. Too weak a dilution will not stop the developer action and too strong a dilution will cause pinholes in the emulsion as a result of the strong chemical reaction to the developer.

(6) Fix only according to instructions. Over-fixing is just as harmful as under-fixing. Be sure, by keeping a usage chart, that the fixer is not exhausted.

(7) Instead of washing the film in running water, rinse by filling and dumping five times with water from the tray. Agitate briefly in each change of water. A solution of Heico Perma Wash or Kodak Hypo Clearing Agent is then used according to the directions, followed by another series of five fills and dumps to clear the film.

(8) A final bath of Kodak Photo-Flo diluted in *distilled* water with 1 ounce per quart of 91% isopropyl alcohol added will give you fast drying, spotless negatives.

(9) Dry immediately in a dust-free place. A shower stall is good, a broom closet is bad. *Don't blow fans or hair dryers on the film;* they will only raise dust which will attach itself irrevocably to the still soft emulsion of the film. Depending on humidity, the film should be dry within an hour, and, with proper storage, will last a couple of centuries.

While not every photographic chemical is deadly poison, they should all be treated as such. Be scrupulous in your cleanliness and rinse every container with hot water after use. Never use the same utensils in darkroom and kitchen. Keep all chemicals away from unsupervised children!

■ *Printing for Permanence.* Old black and white snapshots as well as newly made prints must be properly treated if they are to survive as documents. A treatment in selenium toner and Perma Wash will give archival permanence and will take very little additional time. In fact, Heico states that 5 minutes in Perma Wash bracketed by two 5-minute washes in water is equivalent to six hours of continuously running water. That's a very large saving in time and water, and time and water are both money. ■ Old prints should be checked for fragility. If they are brittle and look like they might not survive immersion for an hour, they should be copied rather than risk floating soggy print fragments down the drain. ■ If you are making your own prints, two fixing baths should be used. After processing each print, fix for half of the recommended time, no more, no less, and place in a tray of water. After three more prints are added, replace the water in the tray with fresh water. Do this every time you add four more prints to avoid a buildup of fixer. When you are finished printing, turn on the lights. *All of the following steps may be done in normal room light.* Refix all of the prints in fresh fixer for the other half of the fixing time. Your old prints should be treated in this second fixing bath. It is much easier if you use your hands to move the prints as tongs are too clumsy. Pull each print from the bottom and place it face down on the top of the stack. Continue this pulling and flipping for five minutes, being careful not to crease the prints as you handle them. When the time is up, put the prints directly into a tray containing the following:

62½ oz. water
1½ oz. Heico Perma Wash (A working solution of other clearing bath may be substituted.)
Add 3½ oz. Kodak Rapid Selenium Toner and dissolve 1½ tablespoons of Kodak Balanced Alkalai.

This solution is good for 25 8 x 10 inch prints or equivalent. Flip the prints constantly in the toner and clearing bath combination for five minutes. ■ *Note: Selenium is a particularly nasty poison. Ensure adequate ventilation and use rubber gloves during the toning process.*

After toning, wash the prints for 20 minutes in running water. ■ There are many print washers available on the market. The simplest and cheapest is no washer at all. A print tray with no more than 10 prints is filled with water, the prints are agitated by flipping once through the deck, after which the water is dumped. Repeat this process for 20 minutes. After that time the prints will be well washed. Next step above the simple tray is the Kodak Tray Siphon, which clips onto a standard tray and blows in and sucks out water. Washing with the siphon is quite thorough, but you must still stand by and flip the prints. More expensive print washers are, of course, available, but keep in mind the key to good print washing is the water exchange rate. Large washers that hold many gallons completely change water every 15 minutes or so. More efficient washers like those made by East Street Gallery and Zone VI Workshop change their water once every minute. The tray methods are not far behind this performance. ■ Selenium is a metal which is much more stable than silver. In the toning bath, the silver particles in the print combine with the selenium resulting in a

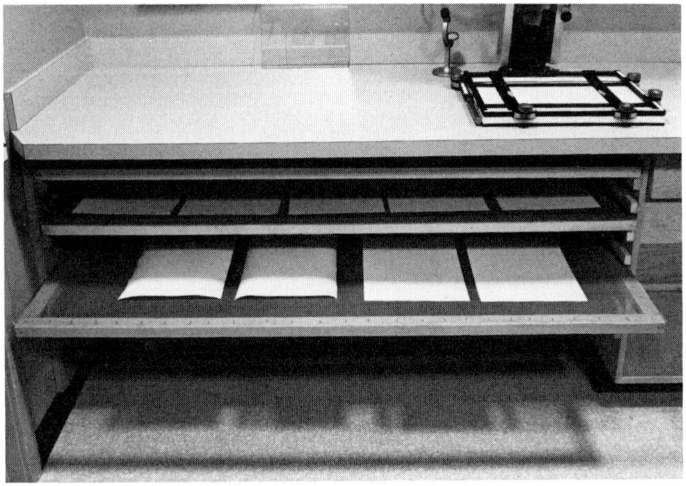

200-year permanence. ■ After the toning bath and 20-minute wash, treatment in Kodak's formula HE-1 hypo eliminator will ensure that all fixer has been removed from the print. As you can see from the ingredients, HE-1 is heady stuff. Use it only in a well-ventilated room, or better, outside.

To 32 oz. water

Add 8 oz. 3% hydrogen peroxide solution
5/8 oz. 28% concentrated ammonia
Water to make 64 oz.

This solution is good for 25 8 x 10 inch prints or equivalent.

Use the HE-1 immediately and then discard. Do not store it to avoid exploding glass bottles. Agitate prints for 6 minutes and follow with 20 minutes of washing.

To recap:
Fix, 5 minutes.
Rinse and store in water until end of session.
Fix, 5 minutes, fresh fix.
Selenium tone and Perma Wash, 5 minutes.
Wash, 20 minutes.
HE-1, 6 minutes.
Wash, 20 minutes.
Dry.

The best method for drying prints with the least risk of contamination is to use fiberglass window screening. Available in hardware stores, it can be stretched on wooden frames or hung, hammock-like, from a windowsill. Prints are placed face down on the screens and should dry overnight. Other dryers invite contamination carryover, but screens are simply hosed down every so often to keep them pure. ■ So-called print flattening solutions are to be avoided. They make the print suck in surrounding moisture and with it, pollutants. Prints will dry nicely flat, unaided on screens. ■ For modern prints, use of the newer resin-coated papers should be avoided. Conventional paper such as Kodak's Kodabromide or Ilford's Ilfobrom, when properly processed, will give you 200-year permanence. The resin-coated papers are so new that there is little information about their long-term storage properties. ■ Not everyone has the space to set up a full-time darkroom, but the procedures just described may be followed in any room, or even outdoors, with normal light. The processes described ensure that existing photographic prints, as well as prints you may make in the future, *will* last for several hundred years.

IV

Organization, Storage and Presentation: For our Great-Great-Great Grandchildren

Where and how you store your family's photographic archives will play a large part in how long it lasts. We face a dilemma here, because we want the images properly stored, but we also want an easy access to them. ■ With the exception of platinum prints and cyanotypes, virtually all commonly used photographic processes involve silver in some form or other. Whether you have an Instamatic or a large view camera, the *film* is all basically the same. Eating a sulphur-laden egg with a quickly tarnishing silver fork will clearly demonstrate that you shouldn't store your photographs with your eggs or where there is any other form of sulphur. Sulphur is everywhere, especially, it seems, in the things we use to store photographs such as cardboard and wooden boxes, rubber bands, rubber cement, wooden picture frames, cheap photo albums and so on and on. The list is endless, and is enough to frighten any good-hearted archivist. ■ Readily available materials can be used, however, to preserve your collection. Polyethylene bags ranging in size from 5½ x 6½ inches to 2½ x 3 feet can be found in grocery stores. The 6½ x 7 inch size is perfect for cabinet cards, and you can see the image clearly without risk of fingerprint damage to the card. Polyethylene sleeves, designed specifically for different sizes of negatives and prints are available from a number of manufacturers (see Appendix). ■ Once all of your negatives and prints are safely nestled in their plastic baggies, the next dragon you must face is the moisture monster. Plastic's one big drawback is that it will keep moisure *in* as well as *out*. Photographs – which are gelatin coatings on paper or glass or film – will, in severe humidity, actually adhere to plastic storage bags. To avoid this, a substance called silica gel is used to absorb humidity. Manufacturers pack little bags of silica gel with cameras and radios to protect them from moisture during shipment. Usually appliance, camera and audio stores will give you silica gel for free; otherwise, chemical suppliers will sell it to you. Place it in the container with your collection to keep it dry. Periodically renew the moisture-absorbing properties of the gel by heating it in a 250 degree oven for an hour. Silica gel should not be placed in direct contact with photographs or negatives – it will scratch them badly. ■ *Proper storage containers for photographic materials should be chemically inert.* Metal filing cabinets may be used, but they must have a baked enamel finish. Fireproof document boxes perfectly proportioned for prints are available in many variety and stationery stores, but you should ensure that the finish is baked enamel. (You *could* bake it yourself.) Government surplus ammunition and

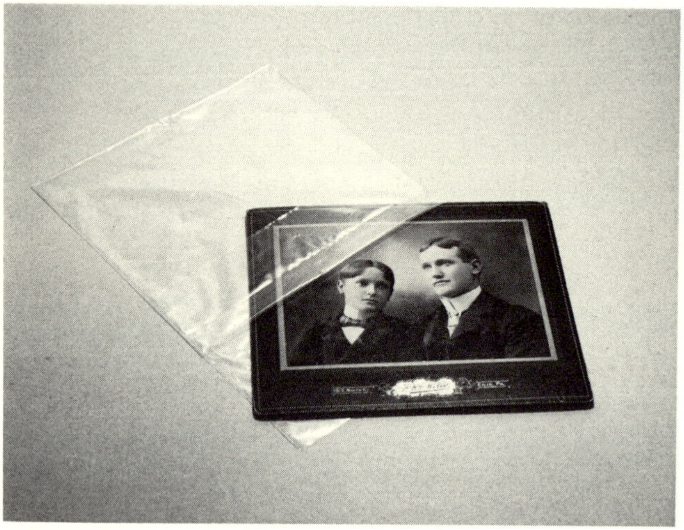

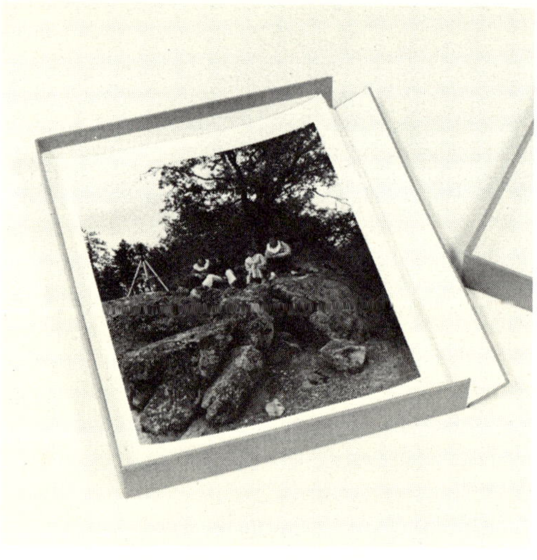

instrument packing cases can fill your needs quite nicely for a relatively small outlay. Negatives and prints in their polyethylene bags, stored with silica gel in hermetically sealed containers will be about as perfectly stored as you can get them. Photographs, like most people, are happiest in cool to moderate temperatures and low humidity. ▣ Photographs are meant to be seen by people. Sealed in a dark vault, the photograph, like the proverbial tree falling silently in an empty forest, ceases to exist. *Pictures must be seen.* Properly done, a photograph will last nearly as long on a wall or in a portfolio box as it will in a steel vault, and will be a lot more useful. ▣ With a growing concern for archival storage of photographs, several manufacturers have begun making print boxes from high quality, acid-free materials. Storage in a box of this type guarantees only that the box will not harm the contents. The photographs themselves must be properly processed and matted to avoid deterioration. ▣ If you are making your own prints, use a larger size printing paper and leave at least a one-inch border around the image area. The white space acts as a buffer zone between the image and the cut edge of the paper where pollutants enter and damage the print. A print in this state, unmounted and stored in its plastic bag, is preserved in the best manner possible. Such a print, however, is subject to damage when handled. We must somehow protect the image, yet allow it to be seen and enjoyed. Matting with proper materials is the first step and proper framing is the final protection. ■ Interestingly enough, custom framers seem to be much more concerned with archival matters than are custom photographic labs. *Once again, the person who cares most about your photographs is you.* Matting and framing is not difficult to do, considering all we've been through. It is best and least expensive if you do these final processes yourself. If you do decide to farm the work out, choose your framer carefully, be sure he understands your concern for archival permanence and has the proper materials on hand ■ A great majority of mat board sold is made of impure materials. Sulphur, that old nemesis, is found in many boards, and acidic components will, in time, make photographs as brittle as old newspaper. ■ Art supply stores are the best place to look for good quality supplies. There are a number of manufacturers of good board, but from experience I can recommend three. Strathmore makes a 100% rag fiber drawing board as well as an acid-free museum board. Charles T. Bainbridge's Sons, Inc. makes a museum board and a light-weight, acid-free barrier paper which is excellent as a protective slip sheet or as archival album pages. The third manufacturer is Rising Paper Company which is distributed by Archival Products. (See Appendix B.) All three make their boards in different thicknesses and in tones from pure white through ivory to a rich cream color which works beautifully with old brown-toned prints. ■ Of the various methods of attaching photographs to mount board, *the very worst is the use of rubber cement.* It is laden with sulphur and will stain a photograph in a very short time. Dry mounting tissue, which bonds photographs to mount board under heat and pressure, is favored by many as the best mounting method. It is permanent and keeps the photograph flat. In addition, it is said to act as a chemical barrier which prevents leeching of harmful compounds from the mount board. I dry mount photographs measuring 11 x 14 inches, and larger, onto high-quality, acid-free board. For smaller prints, I use acid-free photo corners which allow the print to be completely removed from the mat yet keep it flat and safe from harm. Barrier paper is excellent for these corners, as is one-ply Strathmore print paper. Half-inch wide strips are folded (see photograph) and held to the back board with linen tape.

■ The only perfectly safe tape to use is gummed linen tape. At this writing, all other tapes contain harmful ingredients. To be safe, stick with linen tape. ■ In order to hide the corners and to protect the print from

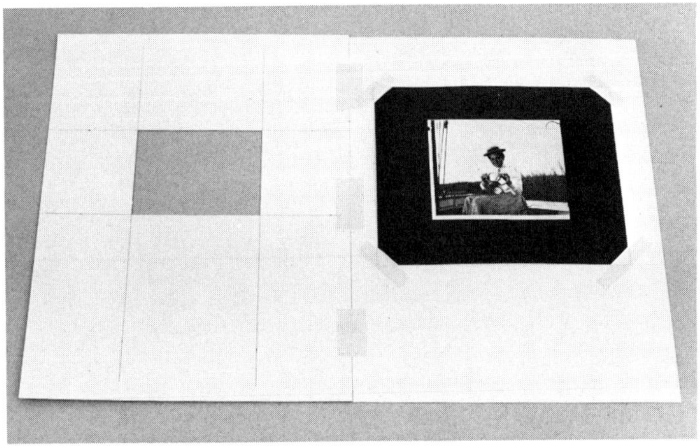

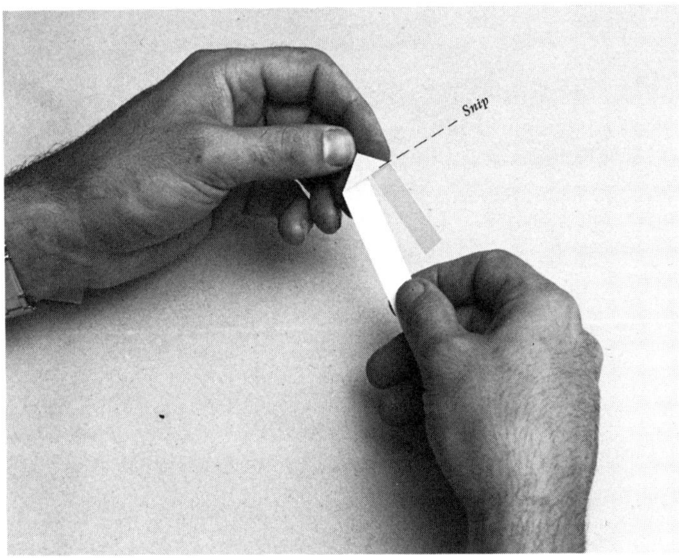

abrasion when it is stacked with others, you will need to hinge an overmat to the backboard, again using linen tape. The cutout, which allows the picture to look out, is most attractive if a bevel cut is used. This can be done with a Dexter mat cutter. It is inexpensive and very easy to use once you've acquired the skill. If you read the directions you'll be way ahead of most people. If there is enough border around the image to allow it, make the window larger than the image. Beveled mat edges are quite sharp and in time can abrade the photograph. If you must have the window the same size as the image, lightly sand the sharp inside edge of the bevel with #400 wet or dry sandpaper to minimize abrasion. For storage in a print box, a piece of barrier paper placed between the print and the overmat will prevent accidental scratching. Placing the print in a polyethylene bag will keep the mat from getting dirty. ■ At this point we are almost back to the dark vault with our photographs. *Pictures are meant to be seen.* Proper framing sets off an image and allows total visual access with very little risk of damage. When framing, an overmat is a necessity in order to keep the print a small distance from the glass. I have seen photographs hung in high-humidity conditions adhere to the glass. The print can be soaked off of the glass, but an ounce of prevention will spare you possible damage to the picture. ■ Wooden

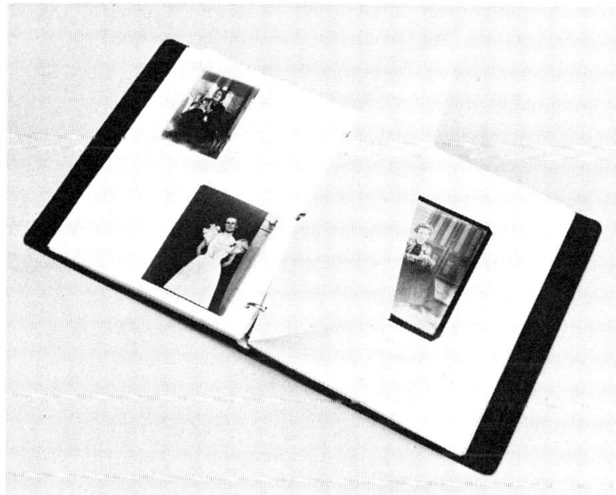

frames (especially bleached wooden frames) are loaded with harmful compounds and are not recommended. If you must use a wooden frame, make a good copy photograph, frame it and store the original. Metal frames are recommended, specifically Nielsen frames. They make a wide variety of styles and all sorts of different colors. Their style #55 is particularly nice, providing a separate channel for the glass that holds it away from the print. This is useful when a protective overmat would cover an inscription. Use glass only when framing – plexiglass may release compounds harmful to photographs. *Do not hang photographs in direct sunlight.* ■ The venerable photo album has undergone many changes. In its present form, plastic pages hold photographs flat and clean. The risk of damage from moisture, however, is great. One album I looked at actually had a warning about possible damage to photographs if they are removed from the album. Cellulose acetate, available as notebook pages, is harmless to photographs, but we still risk damage from high humidity. If, because of young and sticky fingers, a plastic-paged album is a must, use only copy prints. *Best to avoid plastic album pages altogether.* ■ I know of no album specifically designed with archival properties, but one can easily be made. Either Bainbridge barrier paper or Strathmore one-ply drawing paper or print paper can be cut and folded to hold photographs. With paper interleafing, photographs will be unharmed. The use of slits in the pages eliminates the need for photo corners. A three-ring notebook serves as a good binder for the pages. ■ A final method of storage and presentation uses archivally-processed black and white slides. Kodak manufactures a processing kit, Kodak's Direct Positive Film Developing Outfit, that makes slides from conventional Panatomic-X film. The resultant slides are full-toned, very sharp, almost grainless and easily stored. It's about as close as you can get to home-made microfilm. Follow the directions packed with the chemicals and use the procedures described in Chapter II.

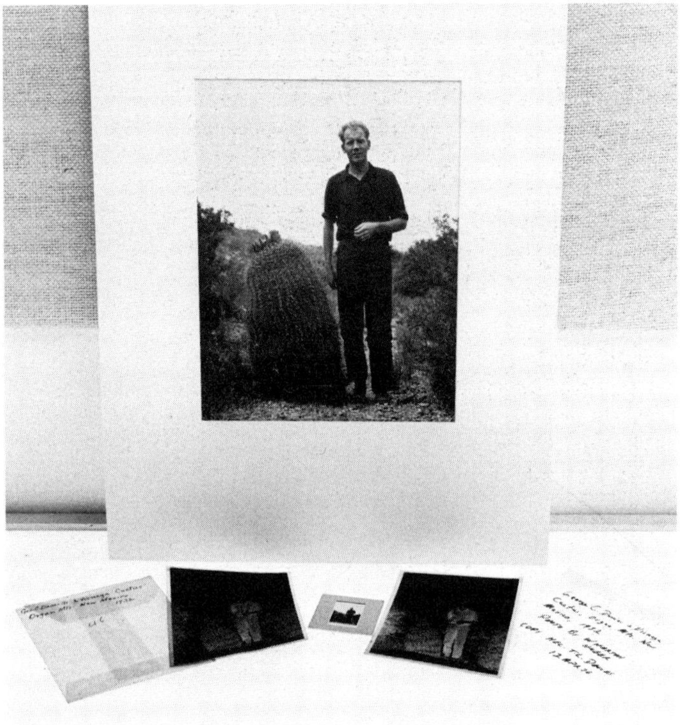

This photograph shows the crumbly glassine envelope, the nitrate negative, a 35mm direct positive copy slide made from the print, an archivally-processed SO-015 copy negative and its acetate sleeve. Note that the negative's description has been carefully transferred to the new sleeve. In the back is a modern print made from the copy negative.

Proper organization of family photographs is vital if they are to be readily accessible. Many people feel that the best way to catalog photographs is to randomly distribute them into ten unmarked boxes. The theory there is that when you want to find a particular photograph, it may take you the better part of a day for the search, but think of the fun you can have looking at all those other photographs you'd forgotten about. I fear many of us fall into this category. ■ If you are just starting to make your history for tomorrow, *you should begin to organize your collection today!* Don't wait until you have several years' worth of photographs piled up: start now. The biggest stumbling block for organization efforts is the prospect of cataloging the mounds of prints from past years. If your collection is small, that hurdle will be easily cleared. If you've decided that now, after 20 years, you're going to get your pictures organized, my heart goes out to you, but persevere; it will be worth the effort. Take it slowly and carefully. It's not an odious task; it's just time consuming. A neatly organized collection is much more likely to survive the ages than is a jumble of confusion. ■ With your prints all around you, arrange them in chronological order. Cardboard boxes with the years marked on the sides – here the 1965 box, there the 1972 box and so on – will serve as temporary organizational bins. If the number of photographs in one box becomes too large, you can sub-divide into months. ■ Once they are arranged in this manner, you should *make a card index,* again arranged by date, which tells when the photograph was made, where it was made and who or what the subject is. A further, but necessary refinement is a cross-reference index which uses keys such as the person in the picture, the place taken, certain holidays, family traditions and so on. The more thoroughly you cross reference, the faster you'll be able to find a certain image. ■ You will want, needless to say, to indicate on the card where each photograph is located in your collection. Each album should have the inclusive dates of the contents prominently displayed for quick access. If you are keeping prints or earlier cased photographs in storage boxes, each box should be marked with inclusive dates. Images that you've chosen to display should show where they are displayed on their card files. ■ Negatives can be stored in metal filing cabinets with bags of silica gel. Roll film and 35mm negatives are best stored in three-ring notebooks for which the negative preservers are punched. Try to store the notebooks with the spine up so the negatives, in their preservers, hang loosely from the rings. This allows more air circulation and minimizes the chances for negatives adhering to the preservers. Sheet film in polyethylene sleeves is easily stored in a card file. Your negative files should show the location of the negative for each print. ■ *Begin now to organize your new negatives.* Store them as above and index and cross-reference each set. A contact print of each set of negatives acts as a quick guide. Don't wait until your negatives turn on you; they will surely trample you to death! ■ Through all of these descriptions two words have constantly appeared. They should be your guides as you work to restore your collection. Repeat to yourself as you work: "gently, carefully." If you become tired or impatient, take a break or stop working for the day. You make more mistakes when you are tired. Measure a chemical incorrectly or slip with a sharp knife and you can destroy a century-old document, not to mention your finger. On the other hand, if you don't take action now, the image might disappear next year. Proceed, but carefully and lovingly.

V

The Current State of Things

The history of photography is full of technical advances eclipsing older processes. The current state of things is no exception, but many fear the worst. Silver, a basic component in the photographic process, is getting scarce. Manufacturers are researching themselves silly trying to find a substitute for silver which would be acceptable to the public. In the meantime, less silver is being used in each piece of film and paper. As a result, it seems much more difficult to produce an acceptable print today than it did five years ago. Resin-coated paper is being improved; it could only get better. Our problem as historians is that we don't know how long RC paper will last. It is best at this point to use conventional printing paper for your family's photo-archives. ◾ Polaroid has a film that should delight the photo-historian. The vast majority of film being shot today is very small in size, either 1 x 1½ inches (35mm), 1 x 1 inches (Instamatic) or the thumbnail size 110 pocket camera film. Imagine, if you will, a film that gives you a print 3¼ x 4¼ inches *plus* a whopping negative of the same size *and* does it instantly. Such stuff exists in the form of Polaroid's Type 665 Positive/Negative film. The negatives are extremely fine-grained and very sharp, but their biggest advantage is their size which will allow small details in the scene to be rendered with great clarity. The print is fully developed in 30 seconds and requires coating for maximum permanence. The negative must be treated immediately in a sodium sulphite solution and rinsed, fix/hardened, washed and dried within three days. Polaroid provides a little bucket that you can store your sulphite and negatives in. You'll fit right in with the kids at the beach. Polaroid does not provide the little shovel. They do, however, provide a packet of sulphite and a measuring cup for proper dilution of the powder. ◾ After the print is developed, separate the negative according to the directions provided with the film. Place the negative in the bucket and let it soak until the black backing becomes slimy and slides off, making the negative visible. When you get home, rinse the negative for a minute in running water. Fix with agitation in Kodak Rapid Fix (with hardener) for 2-4 minutes and rinse for another minute in constantly changing water. Perma Wash for a minute follows and then a 20-minute running water bath, and finally treat with a Photo-Flo/distilled water bath. Hang to dry in a dust-free place. The result is a large negative, full of detail, archivally processed in normal room light, which, if stored properly, will be a valuable document to some future family historian. ◾ It is unfortunate that most of Polaroid's cameras are not on a par with this remarkable film. Their lenses rarely come near the sharpness capability of

Type 665. The sharpest Polaroid, the Model 195, was recently discontinued and no replacement is in sight. ■ The more usual Polaroid prints which have no negatives should be treated as the one-of-a-kind documents that they are. The coating of a Polaroid print makes the image just about as permanent as an archivally-processed conventional print. The coating step seems to be a source of much mess and aggravation for a lot of people. If you squeeze the excess goop from the coater before you coat the print, you'll have a much better looking surface when it dries. Check, by holding the print at an angle to the light, that you've covered the entire surface of the print with the goop. Let prints dry out of people's reach to avoid fingerprints on the surface. ■ A new generation of black and white Polaroid film has eliminated the messy coater, but here again, we are sacrificing permanence for convenience. It appears at this time that the new "coaterless" prints are not nearly as stable as the coated prints. ■ Most color processes are in a state of flux at this writing. Polaroid's Type 108 film pack color surpasses the SX-70 for permanence and both surpass Kodak's instant print process. Rest assured that Kodak is working feverishly to improve their instant film. If you must have color, use Kodachrome film and make or have made Cibachrome prints from the slides. Cibachrome is a relatively new product which is said to have superior color stability. I know that Cibachrome prints can be beautiful, with much of the brilliance and color of the original slide. Ilford, who handles Cibachrome, is about to make available Cibachrome materials to large commercial processors. This will enable you to get Ciba prints from your slides through the corner drugstore. ■ *The secret to long life of color materials is dark and dry storage.* Keeping prints in archival photo albums or in print boxes will extend their life greatly. If you want to display a photograph, display a copy and keep the original in dark storage. If you are projecting your color slides, don't show any slide for more than 30 seconds at a time and be sure that your projector has a heat-absorbing glass between the bulb and the slide. Check your instruction book or ask your dealer. ■ The world of photographic materials is changing tremendously. Some things are getting better; some are worse. Both the instant processes and color processes are being improved rapidly, but they both take a back seat to a properly done black and white negative or print. If the buying public demands permanence, I'm sure the manufacturers will give it to them. But they have to know that you care. Seriously, send them a letter and tell them that you don't want your prints to disappear. Tell them that you are concerned with the archival properties of films and papers. Tell them you want cameras with good lenses that will record historic details with clarity. Why, if we can put a man on the moon . . . (Slow fade, flags waving, music from a brass band up and over.)

Eastman Kodak Company
343 State Street
Rochester, N.Y. 14650

Ilford, Inc.
West 70 Century Rd.
P.O. Box 288
Paramus, N.J. 07653

Polaroid Corporation
549 Technology Sq. Plaza
Cambridge, Ma. 02139

Chairman
Agfa-Gavaert AG
Bayerwerk
Leverkusen
NRW 5090
Federal Republic of Germany

VI
Learning from the Past: The Photographs of Wharton Huber

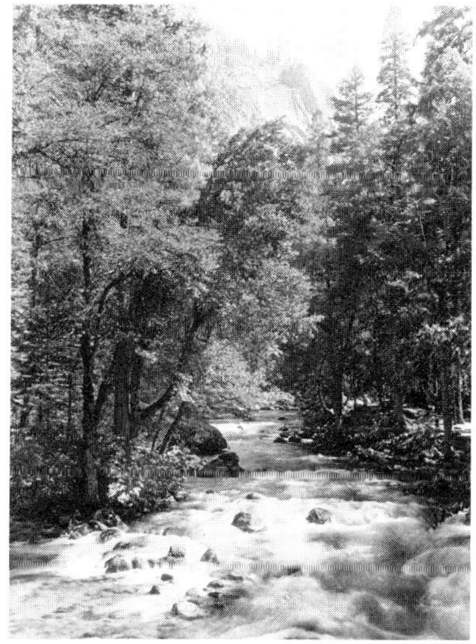

By a stroke of good fortune an unusual collection of glass negatives and prints fell into my hands (gently, mind you) in 1970. The photographer was a friend of my parents, named Wharton Huber. During his life he was a naturalist, travelling widely to collect specimens and to make photographs of birds and animals in their natural surroundings. He was Associate Curator of Birds and Mammals at Philadelphia's Academy of Natural Sciences. Wharton Huber died in 1942, his wife Margaretta died ten years later, but through the photographs they are a real part of my life. Most of what is in this book was learned restoring Wharton's collection. ■ In working with his photographs, I have learned what kinds of photographs appreciate in value over the years. A mountain stream photographed in 1932 looks very much the same today and, barring future calamities, will be that way for centuries. (*Mountain Stream,* Yosemite, 1932.) Now, if that mountain stream were to be funneled into a sewer pipe and paved over with superhighway, we would have an historical document. Elliot Porter photographed a book for the Sierra Club called *The Place No One Knew: Glen Canyon on the Colorado.* In it, beautiful towering rock walls were shown which would normally be visible to anyone for thousands of years. Glen Canyon is now the bottom of Lake Powell, a man-made lake formed by the Glen Canyon Dam. The point is that barring human interference, the natural scene changes slowly and will look much the same 100 years from now as it did 100 years ago. ■ In studying them, we find that photographs which seem mundane when new, gain interest with the passage of time. Wharton's room at Lafayette College (1898) is full of little details: the 45-star flag, the ornate tablecloth, the 'BYSICKLE CHECKING, 10 CT' sign, and a beautiful Vega banjo I would love to reach in and take. This is really nothing more than a catalog of possessions, but they are of another time. *(My Room at College, 1898.)*

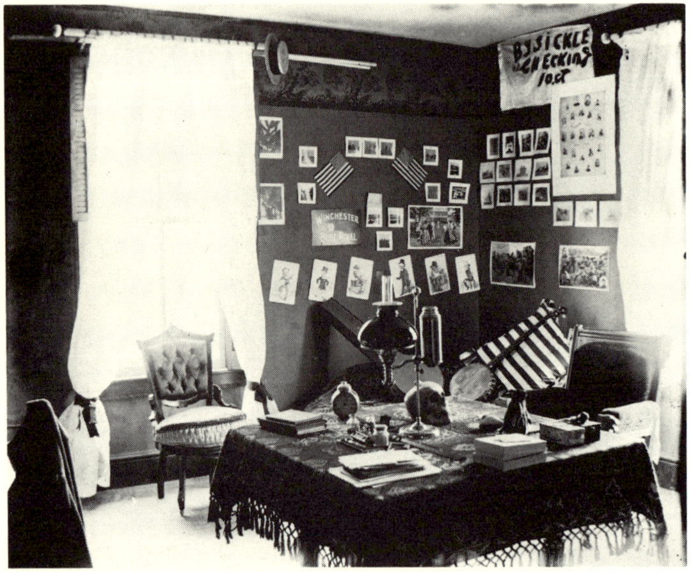

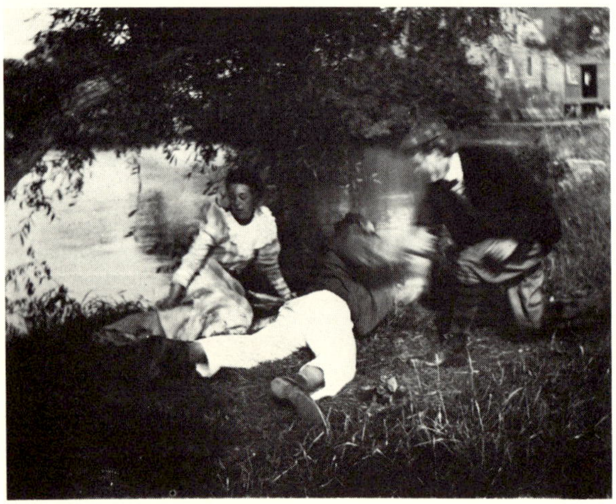

■ One of the photographs on the wall is one whose negative I have found and printed. It is one of my favorites because it is an instant; that fraction of a second will never be repeated. It is anything but a catalog shot; the two men are blurred and detail is lost. This image is a question – we have no explanation of what is happening here. In attempting to explain the picture to himself, the viewer becomes involved personally with the event. The photograph is blurry, but it has a wonderful feeling of the moment that transcends its technical shortcomings. Don't discard technically poor photographs on those grounds alone. Look into the picture to see if it speaks to you. *(Picnic, 1898.)* ■ Another photograph *(Train Station, 1898)* combines the best aspects of both of the preceding images. This one is visually exciting with its unusual angle of view; very few pictures from the 1890s were hip-shots. It is also a fine catalog of clothing details. But the fascination in this picture is the young lady who is looking so directly at us. The thought is mind-boggling – we are looking at her from a distance of 80 years, yet there is direct contact made, almost as if she were talking to us. This is an excellent family snapshot; it has a sense of the moment, yet it is timeless. ■ *A good family photograph should, above all, be intimate.* It should be made by a member of the family. The picture of the *Nicaraguan*

Father and Son (1924) is interesting for its detail, but it was made by an outsider. Pictures made by strangers result in stiff poses reminiscent of the millions of "stand there and smile" family pictures that have been made over the years. *A competent insider has a much better chance for a meaningful photograph than does an equally competent outsider.* ▣ The picture of *Margaretta in the Boat (1905)* is direct and intimate; we are sharing a very quiet, private moment. Yet this picture would not have been made if Wharton had been afraid to take his camera with him. Too many people leave their cameras in the closet for fear of damaging them. The camera was bought not as a closet decoration, but as a tool to make pictures with, so do that. *Carry your camera with you as much as you can.* Not only will you capture some rare moments, but your family will become accustomed to the camera and will not make such a fuss when it is used. ▣ *In most of these pictures we see a simplicity and a clarity of vision that keeps them from being too cluttered.* Too often a photographer will try to get *everything* into one shot: "Here's a picture of Aunt Tilly and the cab driver and the cab and our hotel and the theater we went to and the fountain and the park . . ." Film is relatively inexpensive; don't be afraid to make simple, clear statements. ▣ When travelling, we usually take

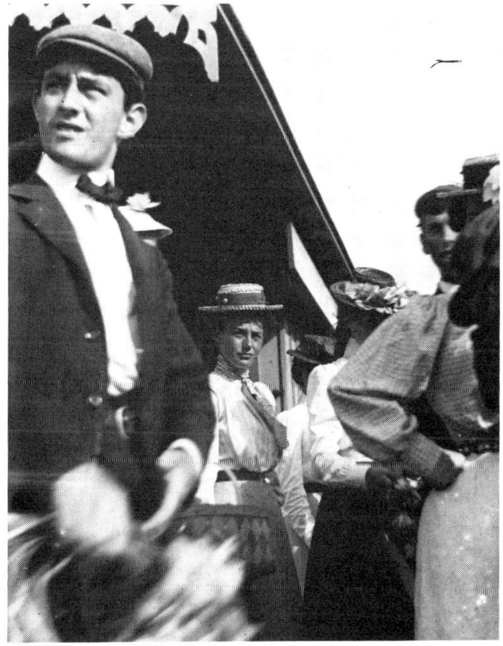

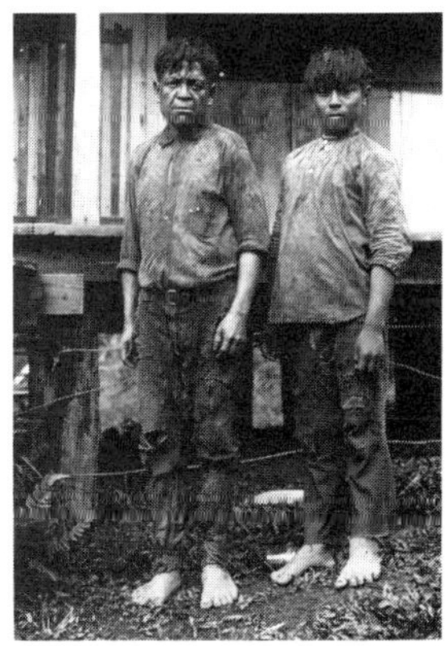

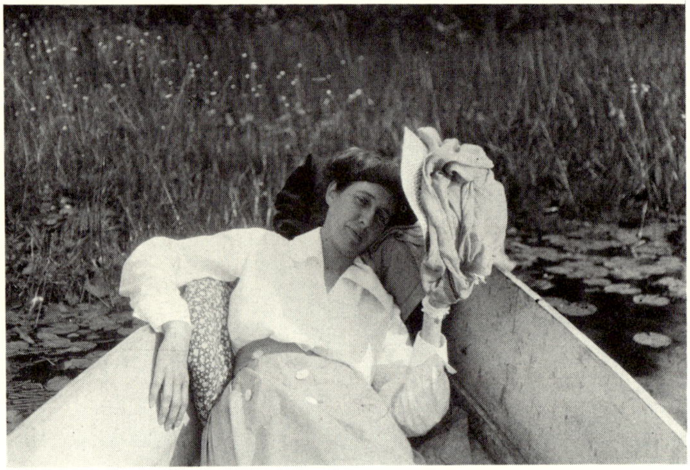

photographs as simple proof that we were there . . . and there, and there. Often we make a geographic reference and little else. Do your audience, present and future, a favor: make photographs that convey a sense of the place. It is not as easy as making a catalog shot, but try, through your pictures, to give the viewer a feeling of what it was like to be in that place; your emotional response as well as your visual record. As we have come to think of ancient Egyptians as constantly looking to the side, hands upraised, so will future generations come to believe we spent our entire lives standing happily in front of monuments. Change that. *Give your descendants something to think about.* ■ Organization of family photographs is up to the family archivist. I prefer a chronological approach, cross-indexed by individuals, event and subject. I find it fascinating to be able to look at my father's life from age two until about a year before he died. The same person is there in each photograph. Again, he is not simply sitting, but doing something in nearly every photograph. Note, if you will, that there is a considerable gap from Dad's wedding portrait in 1934 to the 1959 wedding picture. Where was he? Behind the camera taking pictures of us, that's where. *Don't become so devoted to your task that you become a non-person.* Use the self-timer if you have one on your camera, or better yet, teach other members of your family how to make photographs for the future. Houses, neighborhoods and towns can be photographed in a similar manner. From such pictures we can see how a community has progressed or regressed in its development.

■ Study these photographs and think about the things that make them so fascinating to you. Think also how you can make pictures of your family and travels that will be equally fascinating to someone 75, 100 or even 200 years from now. It is a stab at immortality. *The scenes you see with your own eyes will be seen again and again by future generations.* Through your eyes they will come to know your world. Through your photographs they will know your life.

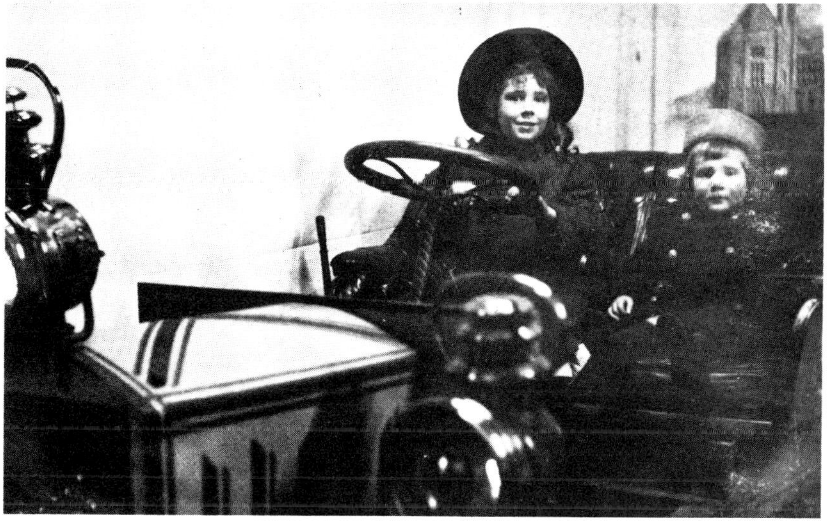

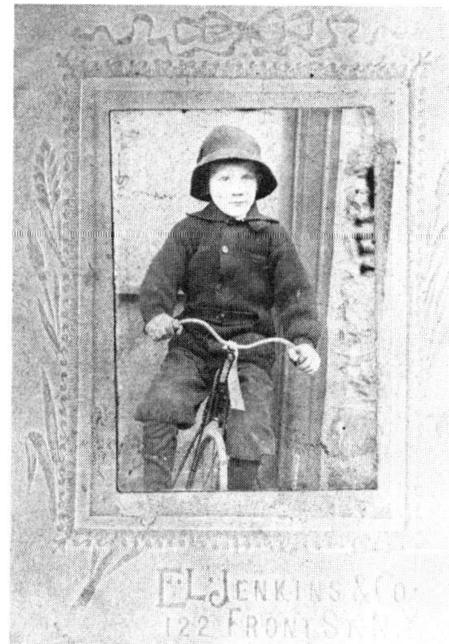
E.L. JENKINS & CO.
122 FRONT ST.

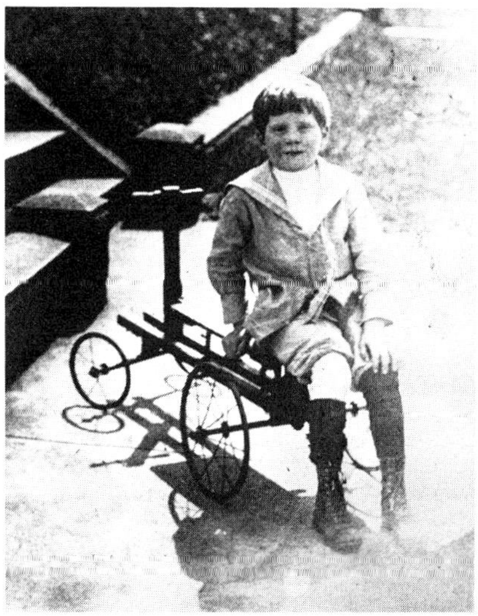

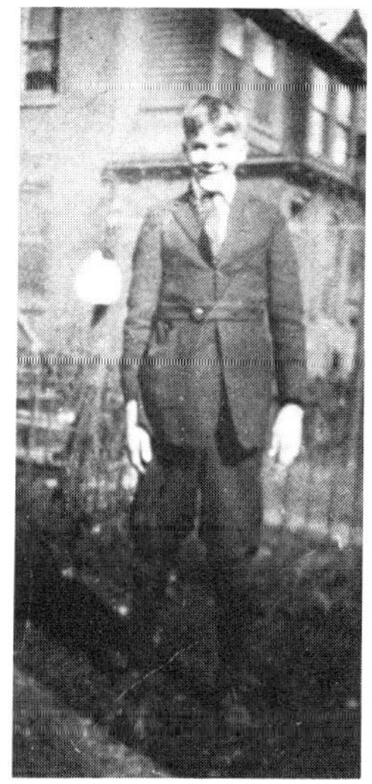

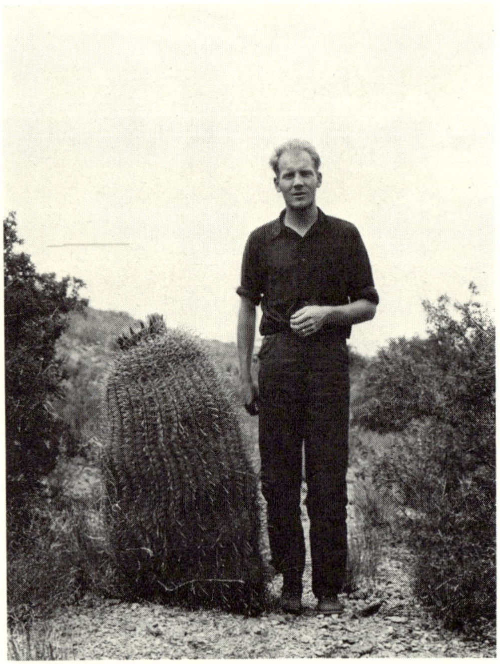

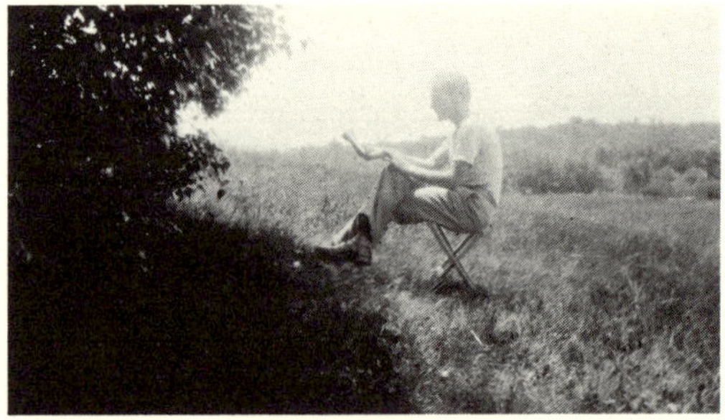

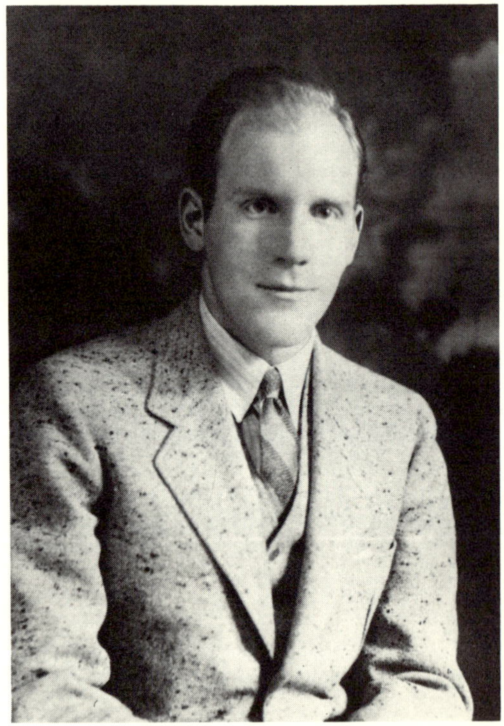

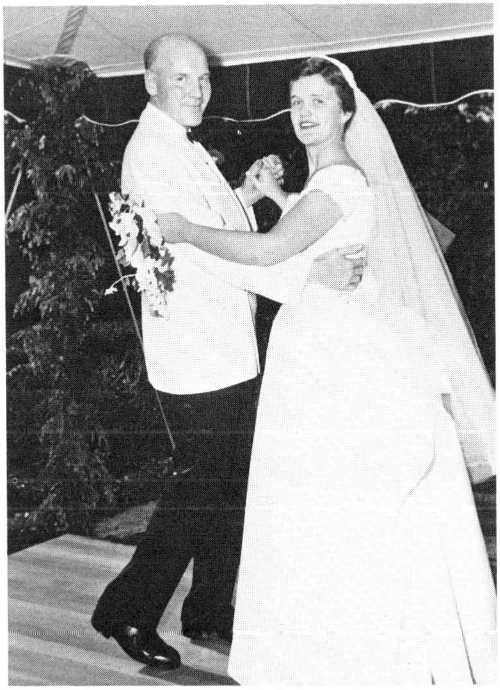

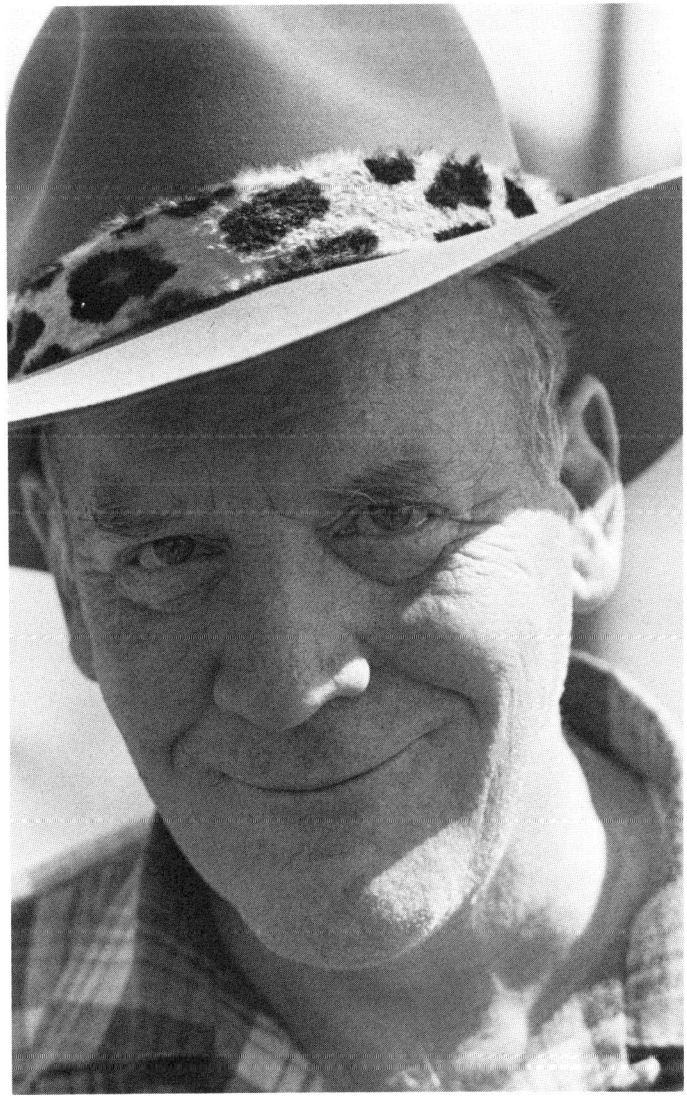

Appendix A
Home-Built Copy Stand

Because copying is an integral part of the restoration process, the photo-historian will surely, sooner or later, have to do some copy work. This home-made setup will make a necessary procedure quicker and easier. ■ The wood should be well-seasoned hardwood in the following dimensions:

Part	*¾″ x 3½″*
A	1 pc. 40″
B	2 pc. 8½″
C	1 pc. 5½″
D	1 pc. 4″
E	1 pc. 3½″
	¾″ x 2½″
F	2 pc. 40″
G	2 pc. 10″
	¾″ Plywood
H	1 pc. 14″ x 17″

Qty.	*Part*
1 pc.	14″ x 13″, ½″ Homosote
20	1½″ #11 Flat head screws
4	2″ #10 Flat head screws
3	¼″ x 2″ Carriage bolts
3	¼″ Wing nuts and washers
3	Spring-type clamps

Assembly is quite simple if you follow the drawing and study the photographs. If you have the wood cut and planed at a lumber yard, be certain that they make all cuts and surfaces absolutely square, otherwise the copy stand will be crooked, leaving you with fuzzy copy prints. ■ The height of parts "B" may have to be altered to place the center of the camera's lens in the center of the 13 x 14 inch copy area. ■ If the camera support is too tight on the rail, a piece of heavy paper, acting as a shim, between piece "C" and either piece "B" will loosen it up. It should slide smoothly, but without wobbling.

The piece of homosote may be clamped to the copy board in order to facilitate holding photographs with push pins. ■ To hold curly photographs flat, a piece of glass must be used. This is clamped over the photograph, but you should be careful of reflections.

A large piece of black cardboard with a hole cut in the center for the lens will effectively eliminate them. ■ This is a tabletop model designed to be used with two photo flood lamps placed on either side for illumination.

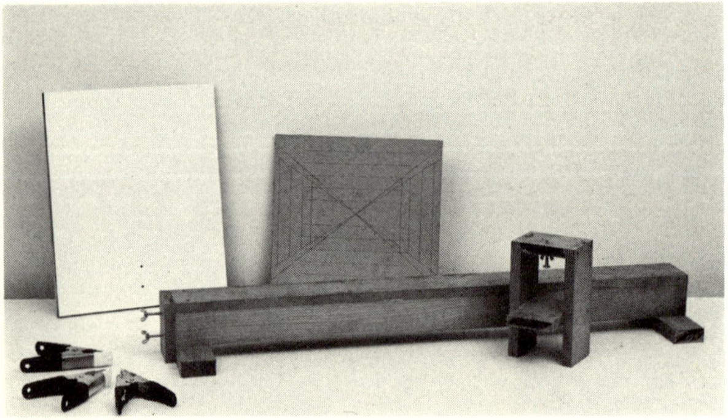

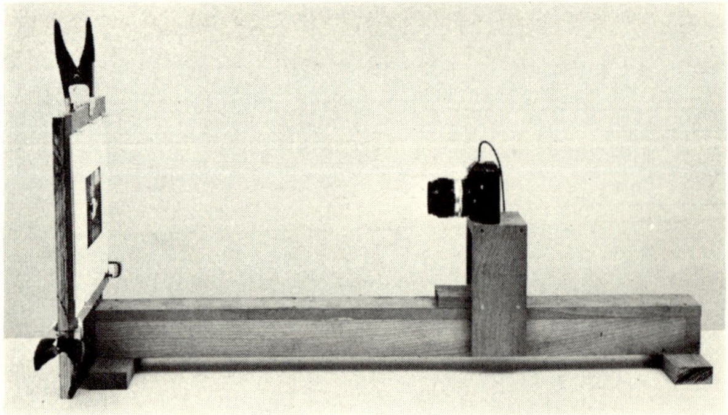

Sliding camera support

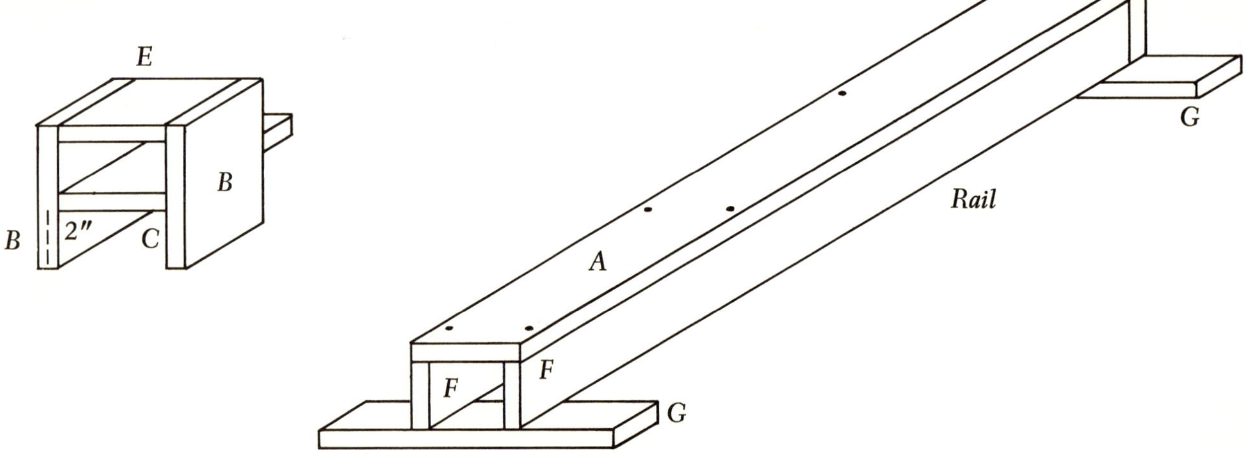

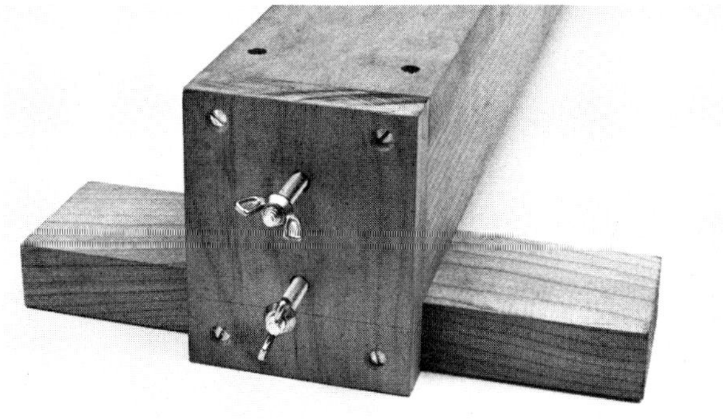

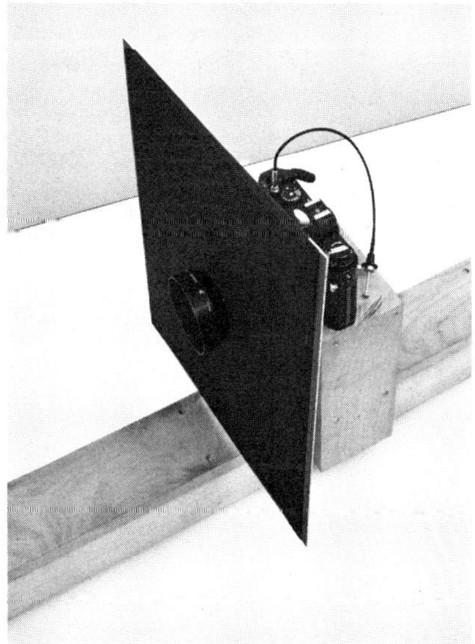

Copy board (H)

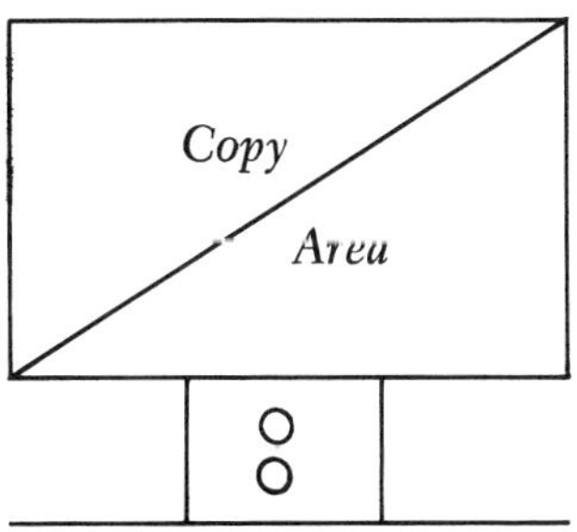

Appendix B
Sources of Supply

Many of the companies listed below are manufacturers who do not conduct retail business. In most cases, they will give you the name of a retailer in your area who carries his product. If you live in Canada, checking with the manufacturer will get the name of a Canadian retailer. Before writing, check with your local art supply stores and college chemistry departments for possible leads. A phone call or two may conserve much time and energy on your part.

Manufacturers

Archival Products, Inc.
Len Hartnett
300 N. Quidnessett Rd.
N. Kingstown, R.I. 02852

Archival products of all descriptions: portfolio and print storage boxes, polyethylene negative sleeves and 100% rag, acid-free museum board.

Charles T. Bainbridge's Sons, Inc.
Bldg. 425, Raritan Center
50 Northfield Ave.
Edison, N.J. 08817

Museum Board

Russell Harrington Cutlery Co.
Southbridge, Ma. 01550

Dexter mat cutter

Heico, Inc.
Delaware Water Gap, Pa. 18327

Perma Wash Archival High Speed Wash

Hollinger Corp.
3810 South Four Mile Run Drive
Arlington, Va. 22206

Print boxes, museum board and negative envelopes

Lewal Industries
65 Plain Ave.
New Rochelle, N.Y. 10801

Instant Dip Silver Cleaner

Morilla Company of California
4552 Colorado Blvd.
Los Angeles, Ca. 90039

Morilla Company of New York
43-01 21st St.
Long Island City, N.Y. 11101

Importers of Fabriano Paper

Nielsen Moulding Design
Townsend, Ma. 01469

Metal section frames in a variety of styles and colors

Retouch Methods Co., Inc.
Chatham, N.H. 07928

Spotone, Spotoff

Strathmore Paper Company
Westfield, Ma. 01085

Strathmore board

Companies Willing to Mail Order

East Street Gallery
723 State St.
Grinnell, Ia. 50112

Archival print and film washers and fiberglass screen dryers. Publishers of an excellent book on all aspects of print and negative preservation (see bibliography).

Edmund Scientific Co.
Edscorp Building
Barrington, N.J. 08007

All manner of apparatus, including polarizing screens for copy work. Great catalog!

Elegant Images
Alan and Devara Goodman
2637 Majestic Drive
Wilmington, De. 19810

Chemicals, papers and other supplies for platinum and palladium printing. Nice people.

Light Impressions Corp.
131 Gould St.
Rochester, N.Y. 14610

A one-stop mail order shopping center for all materials needed for archival preservation. Their 24-page catalog offers print boxes, linen tape, acid-free mounting board as well as matting and framing services which utilize quality board and Nielsen aluminum section frames. They also sell about every photographic book known to man.

Photo Materials Corp.
500 N. Spaulding Ave.
Chicago, Il. 60624

Printing frames

Arthur H. Thomas
3rd and Vine Sts.
Philadelphia, Pa. 19106

Chemical supplies and apparatus. Silica gel.

Zone VI Studios, Inc.
RFD #1
Putney, Vt. 05346

Archival print washers and other supplies.

Appendix C
Bibliography

Technical

Adams, Ansel. *Artificial Light Photography.* Morgan & Morgan. Hastings-on-Hudson, N.Y. 1956.

Camera and Lens. Morgan and Morgan. Hastings-on-Hudson, N.Y. 1976.

Eastman Kodak Company. *Copying.* Professional Data Book M-1. Rochester, N.Y. 1974.

Master Photoguide. Ar-21. Rochester, N.Y. 1974.

Prevention and Removal of Fungus on Prints and Films. AE-22. Rochester, N.Y. 1969.

Processing for Permanence. J-19. Rochester, N.Y., 1970.

Time-Life, Inc. *Caring for Photographs.* New York. 1972.

Vestal, David. *The Craft of Photography.* Harper and Row. New York, 1975.

Weinstein, Robert A. and Booth, Larry. *Collection, Use, and Care of Historical Photographs.* American Association for State and Local History. Nashville. 1977.

Wilhelm, Henry. *Preservation of Contemporary Photographic Materials.* East Street Gallery. Grinnell, Iowa. 1977.

Others to Learn From

Gernsheim, Helmut and Gernsheim, Alison. *The History of Photography.* McGraw-Hill. New York. 1969.

Jensen, Patterson and Belsky, eds. *American Album.* American Heritage. New York. 1968.

Lartigue, Jacques. *Diary of a Century.* Viking. New York. 1970.

Newhall, Beaumont. *The History of Photography.* Museum of Modern Art. New York. 1964.

Porter, Elliot. *The Place No One Knew: Glen Canyon on the Colorado.* Sierra Club. New York. 1966.

Scully, Julia; Miller, Peter. *Disfarmer: The Heber Springs Portraits. 1939-1946.* Addison House. Danbury, N.H. 1976.

Taft, Robert. *Photography and the American Scene.* Dover. 1964.

Index